Quadrennial Defense
Review Report

February 6, 2006

PREFACE v

INTRODUCTION 1

FIGHTING THE LONG WAR 9
   Afghanistan. 9
   Iraq 10
   The Fight Beyond Afghanistan and Iraq. 11
   Humanitarian and Early Preventive Measures 12
   The Department's Role at Home. 15
   Operational Lessons Learned 16

OPERATIONALIZING THE STRATEGY 19
   Defeating Terrorist Networks 20
   Defending the Homeland in Depth. 24
   Shaping the Choices of Countries at Strategic Crossroads 27
   Preventing the Acquisition or Use of Weapons of Mass Destruction 32
   Refining the Department's Force Planning Construct for Wartime 35

REORIENTING CAPABILITIES AND FORCES. 41
   Joint Ground Forces 42
   Special Operations Forces (SOF) 43
   Joint Air Capabilities. 45
   Joint Maritime Capabilities 47
   Tailored Deterrence / New Triad 49
   Combating WMD 51
   Joint Mobility. 53
   Intelligence, Surveillance, Reconnaissance (ISR). 55
   Achieving Net-Centricity 58
   Joint Command and Control 59

RESHAPING THE DEFENSE ENTERPRISE 63
   Toward A New Defense Enterprise 65
   Governance Reforms 65
   Management and Work Reforms 70

DEVELOPING A 21ˢᵗ CENTURY TOTAL FORCE 75
   Reconfiguring the Total Force. 76
   Building the Right Skills 77
   Designing an Information Age Human Capital Strategy 80

ACHIEVING UNITY OF EFFORT 83
   Strengthening Interagency Operations 84
   Working with International Allies and Partners. 87
   Strategic Communication. 91

CHAIRMAN'S ASSESSMENT OF THE 2006 QUADRENNIAL DEFENSE REVIEW. . . . A-1

THE SECRETARY OF DEFENSE
1000 DEFENSE PENTAGON
WASHINGTON, DC 20301-1000

6 February 2006

The Report of the 2006 Quadrennial Defense Review is herewith submitted.

In the pages that follow, the Department's senior leadership sets out where the Department of Defense currently is and the direction we believe it needs to go in fulfilling our responsibilities to the American people.

The 2006 Quadrennial Defense Review reflects a process of change that has gathered momentum since the release of its predecessor QDR in 2001. Now in the fifth year of this global war, the ideas and proposals in this document are provided as a roadmap for change, leading to victory.

PREFACE

The United States is a nation engaged in what will be a long war.

Since the attacks of September 11, 2001, our Nation has fought a global war against violent extremists who use terrorism as their weapon of choice, and who seek to destroy our free way of life. Our enemies seek weapons of mass destruction and, if they are successful, will likely attempt to use them in their conflict with free people everywhere. Currently, the struggle is centered in Iraq and Afghanistan, but we will need to be prepared and arranged to successfully defend our Nation and its interests around the globe for years to come. This 2006 Quadrennial Defense Review is submitted in the fifth year of this long war.

In developing this Quadrennial Defense Review, the senior leaders of the Department of Defense – civilian and military – worked side by side throughout 2005 to:

- test the conclusions of the 2001 QDR;

- apply the important lessons learned from more than four years of war against a global network of violent extremists; and

- test assumptions about the continuously changing nature of the world in which we find ourselves.

There is a tendency to want to suggest that documents such as this represent a "new beginning." Manifestly, this document is not a "new beginning." Rather, this Department has been and is transforming along a continuum that reflects our best understanding of a world that has changed a great deal since the end of the last century. This study reflects the reality that the Department of Defense has been in a period of continuous change for the past five years.

Indeed, when President Bush took office in 2001, the country was in many respects still savoring victory in the Cold War – the culmination of that long struggle that occupied generations of Americans. But the President understood well that we were entering an era of the unexpected and the unpredictable, and he directed a review of the Department of Defense and urged us to transform our forces to better fit this new century.

The terrorist attacks on September 11 imposed a powerful sense of urgency to transforming the Department. Much has been accomplished since that tragic day. We have set about making U.S. forces more agile and more expeditionary. Technological advances, including dramatic improvements in information management and precision weaponry, have allowed our military to generate considerably more combat capability with the same or, in some cases, fewer numbers of weapons platforms and with lower levels of manning. We also have been adjusting the U.S. global military force posture, making long overdue adjustments to U.S. basing by moving away from a static defense in obsolete Cold War garrisons, and placing emphasis on the ability to surge quickly to trouble spots across the globe.

Transforming by Shifting Emphasis from the 20th Century to the 21st Century

The QDR is not a programmatic or budget document. Instead, it reflects the thinking of the senior civilian and military leaders of the Department of Defense:

- Need to "find, fix and finish" combat operations against new and elusive foes.

- Need for considerably better fusion of intelligence and operations to produce action plans that can be executed in real time.

- Realization that everything done in this Department must contribute to joint warfighting capability.

- Central reality that success depends on the dedication, professionalism and skills of the men and women in uniform – volunteers all.

If one were to attempt to characterize the nature of how the Department of Defense is transforming and how the senior leaders of this Department view that transformation, it is useful to view it as a shift of emphasis to meet the new strategic environment. In this era, characterized by uncertainty and surprise, examples of this shift in emphasis include:

- From a peacetime tempo – to a wartime sense of urgency.

- From a time of reasonable predictability – to an era of surprise and uncertainty.

- From single-focused threats – to multiple, complex challenges.

- From nation-state threats – to decentralized network threats from non-state enemies.

- From conducting war against nations – to conducting war in countries we are not at war with (safe havens).

- From "one size fits all" deterrence – to tailored deterrence for rogue powers, terrorist networks and near-peer competitors.

- From responding after a crisis starts (reactive) – to preventive actions so problems do not become crises (proactive).

- From crisis response – to shaping the future.

- From threat-based planning – to capabilities-based planning.

- From peacetime planning – to rapid adaptive planning.

- From a focus on kinetics – to a focus on effects.

- From 20th century processes – to 21st century integrated approaches.

- From static defense, garrison forces – to mobile, expeditionary operations.

- From under-resourced, standby forces (hollow units) – to fully-equipped and fully-manned forces (combat ready units).

- From a battle-ready force (peace) – to battle-hardened forces (war).

- From large institutional forces (tail) – to more powerful operational capabilities (teeth).

- From major conventional combat operations – to multiple irregular, asymmetric operations.

- From separate military Service concepts of operation – to joint and combined operations.

- From forces that need to deconflict – to integrated, interdependent forces.

- From exposed forces forward – to reaching back to CONUS to support expeditionary forces.

- From an emphasis on ships, guns, tanks and planes – to focus on information, knowledge and timely, actionable intelligence.

- From massing forces – to massing effects.

- From set-piece maneuver and mass – to agility and precision.

- From single Service acquisition systems – to joint portfolio management.

- From broad-based industrial mobilization – to targeted commercial solutions.

- From Service and agency intelligence – to truly Joint Information Operations Centers.

- From vertical structures and processes (stove-pipes) – to more transparent, horizontal integration (matrix).

- From moving the user to the data – to moving

data to the user.

- From fragmented homeland assistance – to integrated homeland security.

- From static alliances – to dynamic partnerships.

- From predetermined force packages – to tailored, flexible forces.

- From the U.S. military performing tasks – to a focus on building partner capabilities.

- From static post-operations analysis – to dynamic diagnostics and real-time lessons learned.

- From focusing on inputs (effort) – to tracking outputs (results).

- From Department of Defense solutions – to interagency approaches.

The 2006 QDR in the Context of Continuing Change

The 2006 Quadrennial Defense Review (QDR), above all else, reflects a process of change that has gathered momentum since the release of its predecessor QDR in 2001. A great deal more is underway – all in the midst of a continuing Global War on Terror. A brief summary of some of the work and ongoing initiatives of the Department during this period is outlined below to set the context for the 2006 QDR.

- Liberated more than 50 million Afghans and Iraqis from despotism, terrorism and dictatorship, permitting the first free elections in the recorded history of either nation.

- Conducted attacks against the al Qaida terrorist network, resulting in the death or incarceration of the majority of its top leadership.

- Worked with a global coalition of over 75 countries participating in the Global War on Terrorism.

- Executed urgently needed transformation. As a result of recent combat experience, U.S. Armed Forces today are more battle-hardened and combat ready than in decades.

- Transformed a variety of elements and activities in the Department, including contingency planning, strategic reconnaissance, management of deployments and redeployments, logistics and risk assessment.

- Incorporated hundreds of real world lessons learned from the battlefields in the Global War on Terrorism and adapted the force to ongoing and future operations.

- Initiated a post-9/11 Global Military Force Posture Plan to rearrange U.S. forces around the world, while reducing the Cold War era static footprint abroad, resulting in more expeditionary and deployable forces.

- Reorganized the operational forces, creating Northern Command, with important responsibilities for homeland defense, and merged Space and Strategic Commands into a single command, Strategic Command.

- Initiated a new concept for Army organization, including integrating Active, Guard and Reserve forces around a new modular Brigade Combat Team structure.

- Strengthened U.S. Special Forces by increasing manpower, integrating new technologies, procuring new aircraft, and including the U.S. Marines in Special Operations Forces.

- Spearheaded steps to transform NATO, including enlarging the membership of NATO, enabling the rapid deployment of forces, and extending NATO's role to Afghanistan and Iraq.

- Invested in new equipment, technology and platforms for the forces, including advanced combat capabilities: Stryker Brigades, Littoral Combat Ships, converted cruise-missile firing submarines, unmanned vehicles and advanced tactical aircraft – all linked by Net-Centric Warfare systems.

- Brought on-line an initial Missile Defense System, while continuing research and development, providing a nascent defensive capability.

- Initiated the largest Base Realignment and Closure (BRAC) process in history, right-sizing U.S. infrastructure to future needs.

- Supported the Department of Homeland Security in natural disaster relief for hurricanes Katrina and Rita.

- Undertook massive disaster relief efforts for the South Asia tsunami and the Pakistan earthquake.

- Reorganized the Office of the Secretary of Defense, creating the positions of Under Secretary of Defense for Intelligence, Assistant Secretary of Defense for Homeland Defense, Asisstant Secretary of Defense for Networks and Information Integration and Deputy Assistant Secretary of Defense for Detainee Affairs. Initiated pay for performance and a responsive *National Security Personnel System*. The Department is developing a stronger partnership with the Department of Homeland Security across the spectrum of potential missions.

Conclusion

It is clear we cannot achieve all we might without significant help from the rest of the U.S. government. Within the Executive Branch, we are seeking ways to achieve greater efficiencies in the interagency, in our work with partners in the Departments of State, Treasury, Justice, and Homeland Security, the CIA, and other participants in the Global War on Terror. Still encumbered with a Cold War organization and mentality in many aspects of Department operations, the Department will seek new and more flexible authorities in budget, finance, acquisition and personnel. Now is the time to institute still further changes necessary for the 21st century.

The Report of the 2006 Quadrennial Defense Review represents a snapshot in time of the Department's strategy for defense of the Nation and the capabilities needed to effectively execute that defense. In the pages that follow, the Department's senior leadership sets out where the Department is and where it needs to go in fulfilling our responsibilities to the American people. To realize our goals, the Department stands ready to join in a collaborative partnership with key stakeholders in the process of implementation and execution – the Congress, other agencies of the Executive Branch and alliance and coalition partners. It will take unity of effort to win the long war in which our Nation is engaged. The benefits from such cooperation will be reaped by future joint warfighters, Presidents and, most of all, by the American people we serve.

Finally, it is important to note that this 2006 Quadrennial Defense Review is part of the continuum of transformation in the Department. Its purpose is to help shape the process of change to provide the United States of America with strong, sound and effective warfighting capabilities in the decades ahead. As we continue in the fifth year of this long global war, the ideas and proposals in this document are provided as a roadmap for change, leading to victory.

INTRODUCTION

The Department of Defense conducted the 2006 Quadrennial Defense Review (QDR) in the fourth year of a long war, a war that is irregular in its nature. The enemies in this war are not traditional conventional military forces but rather dispersed, global terrorist networks that exploit Islam to advance radical political aims. These enemies have the avowed aim of acquiring and using nuclear and biological weapons to murder hundreds of thousands of Americans and others around the world. They use terror, propaganda and indiscriminate violence in an attempt to subjugate the Muslim world under a radical theocratic tyranny while seeking to perpetuate conflict with the United States and its allies and partners. This war requires the U.S. military to adopt unconventional and indirect approaches. Currently, Iraq and Afghanistan are crucial battlegrounds, but the struggle extends far beyond their borders. With its allies and partners, the United States must be prepared to wage this war in many locations simultaneously and for some years to come. As the Department of Defense works to defeat these enemies, it must also remain vigilant in an era of surprise and uncertainty and prepare to prevent, deter or defeat a wider range of asymmetric threats.

This QDR defines two fundamental imperatives for the Department of Defense:

- Continuing to reorient the Department's capabilities and forces to be more agile in this time of war, to prepare for wider asymmetric challenges and to hedge against uncertainty over the next 20 years.

- Implementing enterprise-wide changes to ensure that organizational structures, processes and procedures effectively support its strategic direction.

Assessing how the Department is organized and operates has been a centerpiece of this QDR. Just as U.S. forces are becoming more agile and capable of rapid action and are exploiting information advantages to increase operational effectiveness, headquarters organizations and processes that support them need to develop similar attributes. Changes should focus on meeting the needs of the President of the United States and joint warfighting forces, represented by the Combatant Commanders. This QDR sought to provide a broader range of military options for the President and new capabilities needed by Combatant Commanders to confront asymmetric threats. The principles of transparency, constructive competition to encourage innovation, agility and adaptability, collaboration and partnership should guide the formulation of new strategic processes and organizational structures.

The Department must also adopt a model of continuous change and reassessment if it is to defeat highly adaptive adversaries. In this sense, the QDR is not an end state in itself, but rather an interim Report designed to capture the best contemporary thinking, planning and decisions during this period of profound change. The Department will continue this process of continuous reassessment and improvement with periodic updates in the coming years and by directing the development of follow-on "roadmaps" for areas of particular emphasis in the QDR, including:

- Department institutional reform and governance.

- Irregular warfare.

- Building partnership capacity.

- Strategic communication.

- Intelligence.

These roadmaps should guide the implementation of key QDR proposals and continue the refinement of the Department's approaches in these important areas.

The complexity of the challenges facing the Department and the changes needed to address them necessitate a considerably closer partnership between the Executive and Legislative branches of government and continuous dialogue. Without the support of the Congress, it will not be possible for the Department to undertake many of the changes outlined in this Report. The ideas and recommendations presented represent a starting point for such a dialogue. The Department welcomes other viewpoints and innovative proposals from the Congress, allies, and others that build upon these ideas or provide preferable alternatives.

This QDR builds upon the transformational

defense agenda directed by the President and articulated in the 2001 QDR, changes in the U.S. global defense posture and Base Realignment and Closure study, and, most importantly, on the operational experiences of the past four years. In addition to its operations in Afghanistan and Iraq, the U.S. military has conducted a host of other missions, from providing humanitarian relief in the aftermath of the Indian Ocean tsunami and the South Asian earthquake to supporting civil authorities at home and responding to natural disasters such as Hurricane Katrina. Lessons from these missions, which informed the QDR's deliberations and conclusions, include the critical importance of:

- Having the authorities and resources to build partnership capacity, achieve unity of effort, and adopt indirect approaches to act with and through others to defeat common enemies – shifting from conducting activities ourselves to enabling partners to do more for themselves.

- Shifting from responsive actions toward early, preventive measures and increasing the speed

Photo by Photographer's Mate 1st Class Aaron Ansarov, U.S. Navy.

Coalition Forces and local fishermen in the Khawr Abd Allah (KAA) waterway in the Persian Gulf communicate through an Arabic translator. Coalition Forces are working with Iraqi patrol vessels in a joint effort to deny the use of the KAA for illegal activity.

of action to stop problems from becoming conflicts or crises.

- Increasing the freedom of action of the United States and its allies and partners in meeting the security challenges of the 21st century.

- Minimizing costs to the United States while imposing costs on adversaries, in particular by sustaining America's scientific and technological advantage over potential competitors.

Applying these lessons will increase the adaptability of the force when confronting surprise or uncertainty. Maintaining a joint process to identify lessons learned is important to support a process of continuous change and improvement.

The foundation of this QDR is the *National Defense Strategy*, published in March 2005. This strategy calls for continuing to reorient the Department's capabilities to address a wider range of challenges. Although U.S. military forces maintain their predominance in traditional warfare, they must also be improved to address the non-traditional, asymmetric challenges of this new century. These challenges include irregular warfare (conflicts in which enemy combatants are not regular military forces of nation-states); catastrophic terrorism employing weapons of mass destruction (WMD); and disruptive threats to the United States' ability to maintain its qualitative edge and to project power.

To operationalize the strategy, the Department's

senior civilian and military leaders identified four priorities as the focus of the QDR:

- Defeating terrorist networks.

- Defending the homeland in depth.

- Shaping the choices of countries at strategic crossroads.

- Preventing hostile states and non-state actors from acquiring or using WMD.

Although these priorities clearly do not represent the full range of operations the U.S. military must be prepared to conduct, they do indicate areas of particular concern. By focusing on them, the Department will continue to increase its capabilities and forces to deal with irregular, catastrophic and disruptive challenges. Improving capabilities and forces to meet these challenges will also increase the forces overall adaptability and versatility in responding to other threats and contingencies.

Based on their evaluation of the four QDR focus areas, the Department's senior leaders decided to refine the capstone force planning construct that translates the Department's strategy into guidance to shape and size military forces. This wartime construct, described in detail later in this Report, makes adjustments to better capture the realities of a long war by:

- Better defining the Department's responsibilities for homeland defense within a broader national framework.

- Giving greater emphasis to the war on

terror and irregular warfare activities, including long-duration unconventional warfare, counterterrorism, counterinsurgency, and military support for stabilization and reconstruction efforts.

• Accounting for, and drawing a distinction between, steady-state force demands and surge activities over multi-year periods.

At the same time, this wartime construct requires the capability to conduct multiple, overlapping wars. In addition, it calls for the forces and capabilities needed for deterrence, reflecting a shift from "one size fits all" deterrence toward more tailorable capabilities to deter advanced military powers, regional WMD states, or non-state terrorists.

The 2006 QDR provides new direction for accelerating the transformation of the Department to focus more on the needs of Combatant Commanders and to develop portfolios of joint capabilities rather than individual stove-piped programs. In 2001, the Department initiated a shift from threat-based planning toward capabilities-based planning, changing the way war-fighting needs are defined and prioritized. The essence of capabilities-based planning is to identify capabilities that adversaries could employ and capabilities that could be available to the United States, then evaluate their interaction, rather than over-optimize the joint force for a limited set of threat scenarios. This QDR continues this shift by emphasizing the needs of the Combatant Commanders as the basis for programs and budgetary priorities. The

goal is to manage the Department increasingly through the use of joint capability portfolios. Doing so should improve the Department's ability to meet the needs of the President and the Combatant Commanders. Moving toward a more "demand-driven" approach should reduce unnecessary program redundancy, improve joint interoperability, and streamline acquisition and budgeting processes. The Department is continuing to shift from stove-piped vertical structures to more transparent and horizontally-integrated structures. Just as the U.S. forces operate jointly, so too must horizontal integration become an organizing principle for the Department's investment and enterprise-wide functions. These reforms will not occur overnight, and care must be taken not to weaken what works effectively during the transition to a more cross-cutting approach. However, the complex strategic environment of the 21st century demands greater integration of forces, organizations and processes, and closer synchronization of actions.

This environment also places new demands on the Department's Total Force concept. Although the all-volunteer force has been a key to successful U.S. military operations over the past several decades, continued success in future missions is not preordained. The Total Force of active and reserve military, civilian, and contractor personnel must continue to develop the best mix of people equipped with the right skills needed by the Combatant Commanders. To this end, the QDR updates the Department's workforce management policies to guide investments in the force and improve the workforce's ability to adapt to new challenges. For example, to meet the demands of irregular warfare and operate effectively alongside other U.S. agencies, allies or partners, the Department will increase investments focused on developing and maintaining appropriate language, cultural, and information technology skills. The Department is also adopting new personnel systems to reward performance rather than longevity. New joint training initiatives should help ensure that the Total Force is capable of adapting to emerging challenges as the Military Departments continue to rebalance forces between their Active and Reserve Components. Acquiring the right knowledge and skills relevant to the challenges of the 21st century will receive new emphasis in recruitment, retention, training, assignments, career development and advancement. Aligning authorities, policies and practices will produce the best qualified Total Force to satisfy the new demands.

This QDR benefited from the change in the legislation mandating the review. By shifting the completion date of the review to coincide with the submission of the President's Fiscal Year 2007 budget request, the Congress permitted the Department to "front load" a limited number of initiatives into the budget submission for Fiscal Year 2007, rather than having to wait until the next full budget cycle. This QDR therefore recommends a number of adjustments to align Defense plans, policies and programs with the broader strategic direction as "leading edge" measures in the President's budget request for Fiscal Year 2007. These proposals represent only the vanguard of changes that the Department

will initiate in coming years. The Department will develop additional proposals, based on the strategic direction set in this Report, including recommendations for the Fiscal Year 2008 budget submission.

Among the key programmatic decisions the QDR proposes to launch in Fiscal Year 2007 are the following:

- To strengthen forces to defeat terrorist networks, the Department will increase Special Operations Forces by 15% and increase the number of Special Forces Battalions by one-third. U.S. Special Operations Command (U.S. SOCOM) will establish the Marine Corps Special Operations Command. The Air Force will establish an Unmanned Aerial Vehicle Squadron under U.S. SOCOM. The Navy will support a U.S. SOCOM increase in SEAL Team manning and will develop a riverine warfare capability. The Department will also expand Psychological Operations and Civil Affairs units by 3,700 personnel, a 33% increase. Multipurpose Army and Marine Corps ground forces will increase their capabilities and capacity to conduct irregular warfare missions.

- To strengthen homeland defense and homeland security, the Department will fund a $1.5 billion initiative over the next five years to develop broad-spectrum medical countermeasures against the threat of genetically engineered bio-terror agents. Additional initiatives will include developing advanced detection and deterrent technologies and facilitating full-scale civil-military exercises to improve interagency planning for complex homeland security contingencies.

- To help shape the choices of countries at strategic crossroads, strengthen deterrence, and hedge against future strategic uncertainty, the Department will develop a wider range of conventional and non-kinetic deterrent options while maintaining a robust nuclear deterrent. It will convert a small number of Trident submarine-launched ballistic missiles for use in conventional prompt global strike. The Department will also increase procurement of unmanned aerial vehicles to increase persistent surveillance, nearly doubling today's capacity. It also will begin development of the next generation long-range strike systems, accelerating projected initial operational capability by almost two decades.

- To improve the nation's ability to deal with the dangers posed by states that possess weapons of mass destruction and the possibility of terrorists gaining control of them, the Department will greatly expand its capabilities and

forces for addressing such contingencies. It has assigned U.S. Strategic Command as the lead Combatant Command for integrating and synchronizing combating WMD, which provides a focal point for the Department's efforts. The Department will also establish a deployable Joint Task Force headquarters for WMD elimination to be able to provide immediate command and control of forces for executing those missions.

Achieving the vision set out in this Report will only be possible by maintaining and adapting the United States' enduring alliances. Alliances are clearly one of the nation's greatest sources of strength. Over the past four years, the North Atlantic Treaty Organization (NATO) and U.S. bilateral alliances with Australia, Japan, Korea and other nations have adapted to retain their vitality and relevance in the face of new threats to international security. These alliances make manifest the strategic solidarity of free democratic states, promote shared values and facilitate the sharing of military and security burdens around the world. The United States

A soldier of the United Kingdom Black Watch Regiment (center) thanks a U.S. Army heavy transporter driver who has safely delivered his Warrior armored vehicle to Shaibah base, Basra after a long drive south from North Babil, Iraq. Australian and U.S. personnel discuss enemy troop movements during an exercise involving Navy, Army, Air Force, Marine and Special Forces units. The United Kingdom and Australia are key partners in ongoing operations in Iraq and Afghanistan. (Photos left to right)

places great value on its unique relationships with the United Kingdom and Australia, whose forces stand with the U.S. military in Iraq, Afghanistan and many other operations. These close military relations are models for the breadth and depth of cooperation that the United States seeks to foster with other allies and partners around the world. Implementation of the QDR's agenda will serve to reinforce these enduring links.

The 2006 QDR was designed to serve as a catalyst to spur the Department's continuing adaptation and reorientation to produce a truly integrated joint force that is more agile, more rapidly deployable, and more capable against the wider range of threats. Through a process of continuous improvement, constant reassessment and application of lessons learned, changes based on this review will continue over time. Collectively, and with the cooperation of the Congress, these changes will ensure that the Department adapts to meet the increasingly dangerous security challenges of the 21st century.

FIGHTING THE LONG WAR

This war will not be like the war against Iraq a decade ago, with a decisive liberation of territory and a swift conclusion. It will not look like the air war above Kosovo...Our response involves far more than instant retaliation and isolated strikes. Americans should not expect one battle, but a lengthy campaign, unlike any other we have ever seen. It may include dramatic strikes, visible on TV, and covert operations, secret even in success. We will starve terrorists of funding, turn them one against another, drive them from place to place, until there is no refuge and no rest.

President Bush, September 20, 2001

Since 2001 the U.S. military has been continuously at war, but fighting a conflict that is markedly different from wars of the past. The enemies we face are not nation-states but rather dispersed non-state networks. In many cases, actions must occur on many continents in countries with which the United States is not at war. Unlike the image many have of war, this struggle cannot be won by military force alone, or even principally. And it is a struggle that may last for some years to come.

On any given day, nearly 350,000 men and women of the U.S. Armed Forces are deployed or stationed in approximately 130 countries. They are battle-hardened from operations over the past four years, fighting the enemies of freedom as part of this long war. They maintain the Nation's treaty obligations and international commitments. They protect and advance U.S. interests and values. They are often asked to be protectors of the peace and providers of relief. They are a force for good.

Afghanistan

Within weeks after the 9/11 attacks, U.S. and allied forces clandestinely entered Afghanistan and linked up with indigenous Afghan forces. Forces on the ground leveraged joint air power and swiftly toppled the Taliban's repressive theocratic dictatorship. Defeat of the Taliban and their foreign patrons – al Qaida terrorists and their associates – was swift. The war in Afghanistan demonstrated the ability of the U.S. military to project power rapidly at global distances; to conduct operations far inland; to integrate air, ground, special operations, and maritime forces into a joint force; to provide humanitarian relief; and to sustain operations with minimal local basing support. The actions in 2001 in Afghanistan reinforced the principles of adaptability, speed of action, integrated joint operations, economy of force, and the value of working with and through indigenous forces to achieve common goals.

Special Operations Forces ride alongside Afghan Northern Alliance forces during a patrol in support of Operation Enduring Freedom. Special Operations Forces employed local transportation and worked closely with air and space assets to bring precision fires against the Taliban.

Since 2001, U.S. forces have helped to establish the Afghan National Army, to support their first free election in a generation, and to set security conditions for enduring freedom in Afghanistan. Vital international contributions have helped to achieve this result: An International Security Assistance Force (ISAF) of 9,000 military personnel, led by NATO since 2003, operates in Kabul and an increasing portion of Afghanistan's territory, with plans to expand into still more Afghan provinces later this year. As part of the ISAF mission, civil-military Provincial Reconstruction Teams operate in the countryside and undertake reconstruction projects, in coordination with local Afghan officials, to help extend the authority of the central government beyond Kabul and build its capacity for the long term.

Iraq

Much has been accomplished in Iraq since the U.S.-led coalition removed the tyrannical regime of Saddam Hussein and liberated the Iraqi people in 2003: holding free elections, ratifying a constitution, improving infrastructure after decades of neglect, training and equipping Iraqi security forces, and increasing the capability of those forces to take on the enemies of freedom and secure their nation. Although many challenges remain, Iraq is steadily recovering from decades of a vicious tyranny, in which government authority stemmed solely from fear, terror, and brutality. The international coalition is succeeding in setting security conditions for the emergence of a democratic Iraq that will be able to defend itself, that will not be a safe haven for terrorists, that will not be a threat to its neighbors, and that can serve as a model of freedom for the Middle East.

Like Afghanistan, Iraq is a crucial battleground in the long war against terrorism. Al Qaida and its associated movements recognize Iraq as the place of the greatest battle of Islam in this era. As freedom and democracy take root in Iraq, it will provide an attractive alternative to the message of extremists for the people of the region. Success in building a secure, free Iraq will deal the enemy a crippling blow.

> "Victory by the armies cannot be achieved unless the infantry occupies the territory. Likewise, victory for the Islamic movements against the world alliance cannot be attained unless movements possess an Islamic base in the heart of the Arab region"
> -Ayman al-Zawahiri, 2001

Over the past four years, joint forces have adapted to the demands of long-duration, irregular operations. The weight of effort in Iraq has shifted over time, from defeating the Iraqi military and liberating the Iraqi people, to building up Iraqi security forces and local institutions, and to transitioning responsibility for security to the Iraqis.

Iraqi women display their ink stained fingers as proof that they voted.

Iraqi security forces, military and police, continue to grow in numbers and capability. The Multinational Security Transition Command-Iraq (MNSTC-I) has helped create more than 125 Iraqi combat battalions that are now operating with U.S. and other coalition units to find and clear out enemy forces. As more Iraqi units gain confidence and operational experience, they will increasingly take the lead in security operations. This example is a model for the future: helping others to help themselves is critical to winning the long war.

The U.S. Army is harnessing the diversity of American society by recruiting heritage speakers of priority languages to serve as translators and interpreters. A soldier (at the desk with his back turned) is interpreting for his commander at a local police recruiting station in Iraq. To date, the Army has recruited 479 individuals into the heritage speaker program, 133 of whom are currently deployed.

One of the greatest challenges facing U.S. forces is finding the enemy and then rapidly acting on that information. To address this challenge in Iraq, the Department has established in the theater the Joint Intelligence Operations Center – Iraq. This Center integrates intelligence from all sources – imagery, signals intelligence, and human intelligence – and then fuses that information with planning and execution functions to support operations that are often conducted within hours or even minutes of receiving an intelligence tip.

The Fight Beyond Afghanistan and Iraq

The long war against terrorist networks extends far beyond the borders of Iraq and Afghanistan and includes many operations characterized by irregular warfare – operations in which the enemy is not a regular military force of a nation-state. In recent years, U.S. forces have been engaged in many countries, fighting terrorists and helping partners to police and govern their nations. To succeed in such operations, the United States must often take an indirect approach, building up and working with others. This indirect approach seeks to unbalance adversaries physically and psychologically, rather than attacking them where they are strongest or in the manner they expect to be attacked. Taking the "line of least resistance" unbalances the enemy physically, exploiting subtle vulnerabilities and perceived weaknesses. Exploiting the "line of least expectation" unbalances the enemy psychologically, setting the conditions for the enemy's subsequent defeat. One historical example that illustrates both concepts comes from the Arab Revolt in 1917 in a distant theater of the First World War, when British Colonel T.E. Lawrence and a group of lightly armed Bedouin tribesmen seized the Ottoman port city of Aqaba by attacking from the undefended desert-side, rather than confronting the garrison's coastal artillery by attacking from the sea. Today, efforts large and small on five continents demonstrate the importance of being able to work with and through partners, to operate clandestinely and to sustain a persistent but low-visibility presence. Such efforts represent an application of the indirect approach to the long war.

Photo by Senior Airman Latonia L. Brown, U.S. Air Force.

In the Republic of Georgia, a two-year U.S. military train and equip mission with small teams of military trainers resulted in the creation of that country's counterterrorism force. Georgian forces are maintaining security internally and are taking part in Operation Iraqi Freedom.

In East Africa, the Combined Joint Task Force Horn of Africa (CJTF-HOA) is currently helping to build host-nation capacity in Kenya, Ethiopia and Djibouti. Operating across large areas but using only small detachments, CJTF-HOA is a prime example of distributed operations and economy of force. Military, civilian, and allied personnel work together to provide security training and to perform public works and medical assistance projects, demonstrating the benefits of unity of effort. Steps toward more effective host nation governance have improved local conditions and set the stage to minimize tribal, ethnic, and religious conflict, decreasing the possibility of failed states or ungoverned spaces in which terrorist extremists can more easily operate or take shelter.

In the Trans-Sahara region, the U.S. European Command's Counter-Terrorism Initiative is helping regional states develop the internal security forces and procedures necessary for policing their national territories. This initiative uses military and civilian engagements with partners in northern and western Africa to counter emerging terrorist extremist threats. In Niger, for example, a small team of combat aviation advisors has helped Niger's Air Force hone its skills to prevent the under-developed eastern part of the country from becoming a safe haven for transnational terrorists.

Humanitarian and Early Preventive Measures

U.S. forces continue to conduct humanitarian assistance and disaster relief operations around the globe. Preventing crises from worsening and alleviating suffering are goals consistent with American values. They are also in the United States' interest. By alleviating suffering and dealing with crises in their early stages, U.S. forces help prevent disorder from spiraling into wider conflict or crisis. They also demonstrate the goodwill and compassion of the United States.

In the eastern Indian Ocean, the U.S. military was at the vanguard of an international effort to provide relief to stranded victims of the disastrous December 2004 tsunami. The U.S. Pacific Command and U.S. Transportation Command responded rapidly, deploying a Joint Task Force to Thailand, Indonesia and Sri Lanka within five days of the catastrophe. Strategic airlift, supplemented by the arrival of an aircraft carrier, amphibious ships, and a hospital ship provided urgent relief. These forces maintained 24-hour operations and helped coordinate the various international relief efforts. Over a six-week period, U.S. forces airlifted over 8,500 tons of critical emergency supplies to isolated and previously unreachable areas, conducted search and rescue operations and treated more than 10,000 patients.

Photo by Photographer's Mate 1st Class Bart A. Bauer, U.S. Navy.

A Landing Craft Air Cushioned (LCAC) crew assigned to the USS Bonhomme Richard unloads humanitarian relief supplies in the city of Meuloboh, on the island of Sumatra, Indonesia. U.S. military elements quickly responded to provide aid to victims of the December 2004 Indian Ocean tsunami.

Similarly, in October 2005, when a devastating earthquake struck northern Pakistan, U.S. forces proved their adaptability by responding within eighteen hours. U.S. military aircraft, among the first on the scene, transported and distributed humanitarian supplies throughout the affected areas. A combined Pakistani-U.S. Civil-Military Disaster Assistance Center seamlessly integrated contributions from various nations and international aid organizations. U.S. strategic airlift augmented the capacity of partner countries by transporting relief personnel and supplies from across the globe to Pakistan. Deployable U.S. military field hospitals were quickly established to supplement damaged Pakistani medical facilities, and U.S. military engineers helped to re-open hundreds of miles of roads, permitting the flow of aid to remote communities.

Photo by Technical Sergeant Mike Buytas, U.S. Air Force.

Pakistani earthquake victims crowd around a U.S. Army CH-47 Chinook helicopter delivering disaster relief supplies to the devastated area surrounding the town of Oghi, Pakistan. The U.S. military participated in the multinational effort to provide humanitarian assistance after the October 2005 earthquake.

Over the past four years, U.S. forces have also played critical roles preventing crises from becoming more serious conflicts. In Liberia in 2003, civil war and the dissolution of the government prompted a multinational intervention to restore order and prevent a full-blown humanitarian crisis. A U.S. European Command joint task force accompanied a force from the Economic Community of West African States (ECOWAS) throughout the mission. The U.S. team, working with regional partners, secured and re-opened the country's major seaport to permit the flow of humanitarian assistance. The United States and ECOWAS succeeded in stabilizing the country, permitting a rapid turnover of humanitarian assistance responsibility to the United Nations in support of the new interim Liberian government.

Similarly, in response to increasing political violence in Haiti in early 2004, U.S. joint forces rapidly deployed as part of a multinational stabilization force. This early action prevented the collapse of political and social structures

The commander of U.S. forces under Joint Task Force Liberia speaks with soldiers from Ghana, one of the West African countries that led the effort to stabilize Liberia. With the arrival of West African forces, the security environment and humanitarian conditions in Liberia improved significantly.

in the country, averted a humanitarian crisis, and established a more secure and stable environment, which enabled the speedy transfer of responsibility for supporting the Haitian transitional government to the United Nations.

U.S. Southern Command's support for Plan Colombia is yet another example of preventive action. The United States has worked with the Government of Colombia to combat the production and trafficking of illegal drugs. In 2002, at the request of the Administration, Congress granted expanded authorities to help the Colombian Government wage a unified campaign against terrorism as well as drugs, and thereby assert effective control over its territory. This broader mission has helped the Colombian Government seize the initiative against illegal armed groups, demobilize thousands of illegal paramilitaries, decrease violence and return to government authority areas that had been under the control of narcoterrorists for decades.

Integrated joint operations have also played critical roles in deterring conflict and preserving

stability in the Pacific. Forward-deployed forces and flexible deterrent options have successfully dissuaded potential enemies and assured allies and partners. During operations in Iraq in the spring of 2003, regional deterrence capabilities and global repositioning of joint forces and precision munitions demonstrated U.S. resolve and commitment to maintaining the armistice on the Korean Peninsula.

Highly distributed global operations over the past several years – in the Pacific and Indian Oceans, Central Asia, the Middle East, the Caucasus, the Balkans, Africa, and Latin America – make manifest the importance of small teams conducting missions uniquely tailored to local conditions. These operations also demonstrate the agility of U.S. forces forward-deployed in and near these regions to transition quickly from deterrence to humanitarian or other operations as required. In some places, U.S. forces have concentrated on attacking and disrupting enemy forces. In others, U.S. forces have worked to improve the lives of people in impoverished regions, or to build up the capacity of local security forces to police their own countries. In almost all cases, updated authorities, processes and practices were required to ensure unity of effort in these distributed operations. Still, additional cooperation authorities will be required if the U.S. Government is to be able to achieve its goals in the most cost-effective manner.

Recent operations have reinforced the need for U.S. forces to have greater language skills and cultural awareness. It is advantageous for U.S. forces to speak the languages of the regions

Photo by Technical Specialist
John M. Foster, U.S. Air Force.

During the exercise New Horizons 2005 in El Salvador, U.S. Army personnel describe preventive health measures to local citizens. New Horizons included a civic action project which provided medical assistance visits, two new schools and three clinics in areas hit by earthquakes in 2004.

where the enemy will operate. In 2004, the Department of Defense launched the Defense Language Transformation Initiative to improve the ability of the Armed Forces to work more effectively with international partners. The Military Departments have also begun more intensive cultural and language training, which over time will create a more culturally aware, linguistically capable force, better able to forge victory in the long war. The Department must overcome a legacy of relatively limited emphasis on languages and continue to expand efforts to place linguistically capable individuals at all levels of the military – from the tactical squad to the operational commander.

The Department's Role at Home

The long war has also seen U.S. forces taking on greater roles at home. Immediately following the 9/11 attacks, U.S. forces were called upon to assist in securing the homeland. Working with other Federal agencies, the Department

answered the call. At the President's direction, active and reserve forces conducted combat air patrols over major cities to prevent follow-on attacks, reinforced the Nation's land borders, guarded shipping lanes, protected harbors, secured critical infrastructure, and guarded airports and other transportation hubs until the establishment of the Transportation Security Administration. Specialized anti-terrorism and chemical and biological incident response forces deployed to Washington, D.C. in the wake of the 2001 anthrax attacks.

The Department has undertaken a number of major changes to strengthen its ability to defend the homeland and support civil authorities. In 2002, the Department created a new Combatant Command, U.S. Northern Command (U.S. NORTHCOM), with the responsibility to consolidate homeland defense missions under a single headquarters. To coordinate its efforts and to increase the emphasis on homeland defense issues, the Department established the new civilian post of Assistant Secretary of Defense for Homeland Defense.

The Department has played an active role in Federal efforts to shore up defenses against the threat of biological terrorism. It is helping to develop vaccines for Project BioShield, a national effort to accelerate the development of medical counter-measures to defend against potential biological attacks. In Project BioWatch, the Department collaborates with other Federal agencies on improving technologies and procedures to detect and identify biological attacks. In 2004, the Department led the establishment of the National BioDefense Campus at Fort Detrick, Maryland, which provides a means for coordination among agencies working on research and development of medical biological defenses.

At the state level, the National Guard is fielding 55 WMD Civil Support Teams (CSTs) – in each state, territory and the District of Columbia. These 22-member teams can provide critical communications links, quick assessment of damage from any WMD attack and consequence management support to local, state and Federal agencies. The National Guard is also creating twelve Enhanced Response Force Packages for chemical, biological, radiological, nuclear and high-yield explosive attacks. These units provide capabilities to locate and extract victims from a WMD-contaminated environment, to conduct casualty and patient decontamination and to provide medical treatment. To improve command and control functions for emergencies and major public events, the National Guard is creating a Joint Force Headquarters in each state.

Just as they have proved adaptable in providing rapid response to disasters abroad, U.S. forces have been called upon to respond to natural disasters at home. In the wake of Hurricane Katrina, pre-positioned forces arrived in neighborhoods of Gulf Coast communities within four hours after the storm hit, to assist rescue efforts. More than 50,000 National Guard personnel deployed to the disaster zone. Active forces added an additional 22,000 personnel, including units previously deployed to Afghanistan and Iraq. Together, working with the Coast Guard, they conducted

An Air Force fire truck is loaded onto a C-130 Hercules bound for Mississippi during Hurricane Katrina relief efforts. The U.S. Air Force personnel are from the 162nd Fighter Wing, Arizona Air National Guard.

search and rescue missions, evacuations, and medical airlift from the air, land, and sea. The Department's response to Hurricane Katrina and other civil support operations provided valuable lessons for improving force integration and command and control in large, complex interagency operations.

Operational Lessons Learned

Operational experiences – in Afghanistan and Iraq, in wider operations as part of the war on terror, in humanitarian relief efforts and preventive actions and in the Department of Defense's role at home – have provided important lessons and principles that the Department has already begun to apply. These overarching lessons have broad applicability to many of the challenges the Department faces. They have informed the new approaches developed during the QDR aimed at continuing the reorientation of military capabilities and implementing enterprise-wide reforms to ensure that structures and processes support the warfighter. They include:

- Having the Authorities and Resources to Build Partnership Capacity. Recent operations demonstrate the critical importance of being organized to work with and through others, and of shifting emphasis from performing tasks ourselves to enabling others. They also underscore the importance of adopting a more indirect approach to achieve common objectives. The Department must help partners improve their ability to perform their intended roles and missions. This includes foreign governments trying to police themselves and govern their populations more justly and effectively; at home, it includes other Federal agencies and state and local governments. The U.S. military's interaction with foreign militaries provides valuable opportunities to expand partner capacity as well as to establish trust and build relationships. Recent efforts to build partnership capacity also highlight the importance of flexible access to funding through programs such as the Commander's Emergency Response Program (CERP) and Train and Equip authorities for operations in Iraq and Afghanistan. Expanding authorities to build on the lessons learned in Iraq and Afghanistan will help enable the United States to defeat terrorist networks wherever they are located. Congress is urged to work alongside the Department to provide the full set of authorities needed to build security partnerships to fight the war on terror. In addition to the recently enacted authority to Build the Capacity of Foreign Military Forces and Emergency Transfer Authority for the State Department's Coordinator for Reconstruction and Stabilization amendments, needed authorities include: institutionalizing CERP for named contingency operations *world-wide;* expanding the President's authority to task and resource best-situated Federal agencies in an emergency; and broader reimbursement authority for coalition support forces and expanded logistics support to other nations partnering with the United States in the war on terror.

Members of Task Force Phoenix, Indiana National Guard (center), conduct an after-action review with Afghan National Army soldiers. With the aid of U.S. forces, Afghan soldiers are becoming increasingly self-sufficient.

- Taking Early Preventive Measures. Drawing on lessons from recent operations, the QDR emphasized the importance of early measures to prevent problems from becoming crises and crises from becoming conflicts. Operations in Haiti and Liberia demonstrate the advantage of taking prompt action to quell disorder before it leads to the collapse of political and social structures. Those operations help set conditions for the restoration of security and civil society. Taking early measures requires greater speed of action and a clear understanding of the situation, including the way potential adversaries make decisions. In many recent counterterrorist operations, the time available to apprehend a terrorist, once located, has been measured in mere minutes. Similarly, as the terrorist attacks on September 11, 2001 showed, defending the homeland against air or missile attacks with little or no warning also requires the ability to act on very short notice. U.S. forces have demonstrated time and again their agility in responding rapidly to crises. However, operational agility has not yet been matched by the availability of sufficiently broad authorities or the processes and procedures needed to support the warfighter. In a number of recent operations, the lack of needed authorities hindered the ability of U.S. forces to act swiftly, and the process to get appropriate authorities has often taken months to achieve.

- Increasing Freedom of Action. Recent operations also reinforce the need to increase the freedom of action and the range of options available to the United States, as well as its allies and partners, to address the security challenges of the 21st century. The ability of U.S. and allied forces to conduct operations in land-locked Afghanistan only weeks after the 9/11 attacks demonstrated the value of operational readiness and global reach. Building partnership capacity and strengthening alliances to defeat terrorist networks is an example of how the United States can strengthen freedom of action at the strategic level. The QDR proposes measures to increase both strategic and operational freedom of action by combining a more indirect approach, stealth, persistence, flexible basing and strategic reach.

- Shifting Cost Balances. For a few hundred thousand dollars and the lives of nineteen terrorists, on September 11, 2001, al Qaida murdered some 3,000 people and inflicted enormous economic costs on the United States. In confronting the range of security challenges it will face in the 21st century, the United States must constantly strive to minimize its own costs in terms of lives and treasure, while imposing unsustainable costs on its adversaries. The United States, NATO, other allies and partners can impose costs by taking actions and making investments that complicate an adversary's decision-making or promote self-defeating actions. Effective cost-imposing strategies also heighten an adversary's sense of uncertainty, potentially creating internal fissures in its leadership. Sustaining America's scientific and technological advantages over any potential competitor contributes to the nation's ability to dissuade future forms of military competition.

The Department applied these lessons over the course of the QDR as it identified changes to the mix of joint capabilities and the enterprise-wide reforms needed to fight the long war.

OPERATIONALIZING THE STRATEGY

The *National Defense Strategy*, published in March 2005, provides the strategic foundation of the QDR. The strategy acknowledges that although the U.S. military maintains considerable advantages in traditional forms of warfare, this realm is not the only, or even the most likely, one in which adversaries will challenge the United States during the period immediately ahead. Enemies are more likely to pose asymmetric threats, including irregular, catastrophic and disruptive challenges. Some, such as non-state actors, will choose irregular warfare – including terrorism, insurgency or guerrilla warfare – in an attempt to break our will through protracted conflict. Some states, and some non-state actors, will pursue WMD to intimidate others or murder hundreds of thousands of people. Finally, some states may seek capabilities designed to disrupt or negate traditional U.S. military advantages.

To operationalize the *National Defense Strategy*, the Department's senior civilian and military leaders identified four priority areas for examination during the QDR:

- Defeating terrorist networks.

- Defending the homeland in depth.

- Shaping the choices of countries at strategic crossroads.

- Preventing hostile states and non-state actors from acquiring or using WMD.

These inter-related areas illustrated the types of capabilities and forces needed to address the challenges described in the *National Defense Strategy*. They helped the Department to assess that strategy and review its force planning construct.

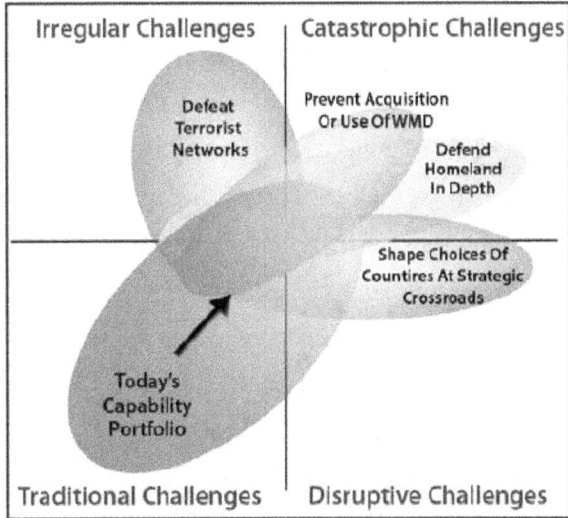

As the diagram shows, the Department is shifting its portfolio of capabilities to address irregular, catastrophic and disruptive challenges while sustaining capabilities to address traditional challenges.

Although these focus areas do not encompass the full range of military activities the Department may have to conduct, senior leaders identified them as among the most pressing problems the Department must address. All of them have both near-term and long-term implications. In all four areas, there are immediate measures that can be put in place to reduce near-term risks while other measures are being developed to increase the range of options available in the future. Strengthening capabilities in these areas will also improve the versatility of the force to perform a wider range of military operations than today.

Senior leaders considered the nature of each problem, identified desired objectives in each area and developed approaches for achieving those objectives. The focus areas helped to identify the capabilities that are needed to continue the reorientation of the joint force over time. These changes will not occur all at once, but will be part of a process of continuous change.

Common to all of the focus areas is the imperative to work with other government agencies, allies and partners and, where appropriate, to help them increase their capacities and capabilities and the ability to work together. In all cases, the four focus areas require the application of multiple elements of national power and close cooperation with international allies and partners. The Department cannot solve these problems alone. The QDR proposes, therefore, that the United States strengthen existing alliances and develop new partnerships to address common threats. Through these partnerships, the Department can assist others in developing the wherewithal to protect their own populations and police their own territories, as well as to project and sustain forces to promote collective security.

Photo by Sergeant Jeremy Clawson, U.S. Army.

An Army reservist with the Herat Provisional Reconstruction Team visits children at a local orphanage. Working on Provincial Reconstruction Teams alongside personnel from the U.S. State Department, NATO and other allies, U.S. forces are bringing a sense of normalcy to remote areas of Afghanistan.

This chapter outlines each of the four focus areas. It then describes the refinement of the Department's force planning construct to better align the shape and size of U.S. forces to address these new challenges and to conduct the full range of military operations.

Defeating Terrorist Networks

The rise of global non-state terrorist networks is one of the defining characteristics of the last decade. The enemies we face are not traditional conventional military forces, but rather distributed multi-national and multi-ethnic networks of terrorists. These networks seek to break the will of nations that have joined the fight alongside the United States by attacking their populations. Terrorist networks use intimidation, propaganda and indiscriminate violence in an attempt to subjugate the Muslim world under a radical theocratic tyranny. These networks also aim to exhaust the will of the United States and its allies and partners, including those in the Muslim world, to oppose them. Terrorist networks seek ever deadlier means, including nuclear and biological weapons, to commit mass murder.

> *"The jihad movement must adopt its plan on the basis of controlling a piece of land in the heart of the Islamic world on which it could establish and protect the state of Islam and launch its battle to restore the rational caliphate based on the traditions of the prophet."*
> *- Ayman al-Zawahiri, 2001*

For the past several decades, al Qaida and its associated movements have focused their efforts on their "near enemy": moderate governments throughout the greater Middle East. In the 1990s, they shifted toward attacking their "far enemy": the United States and other western powers – in an attempt to change the character of the conflict, galvanize pan-Islamic support, bleed the United States (as the Mujahideen had done to the Soviet Union in Afghanistan during the 1980s), and weaken Western support for Middle Eastern governments. They use terrorist attacks to perturb the international community and trigger actions that could strengthen their position and move them closer toward their objectives.

Such terrorist networks oppose globalization and the expansion of freedom it brings. Paradoxically, they use the very instruments of globalization – the unfettered flow of information and ideas, goods and services, capital, people and technology – as their preferred means of attack. They target symbols of modernity like skyscrapers with civilian jetliners used as missiles. They exploit the Internet as a cyber-sanctuary, which enables the transfer of funds and the cross-training of geographically isolated cells. They use cell phones and text messaging to order attacks and detonate car bombs. They send pre-recorded video messages to sympathetic media outlets to distribute their propaganda "free of charge" and to spread their ideology of hate. They encourage terrorist "startup franchises" around the world that conduct attacks in copy-cat fashion. They depend on 24/7 news cycles for the publicity they seek to attract new recruits. They plan to attack targets from safe-houses half a world away. They seek weapons of mass destruction from transnational proliferation networks.

A U.S. soldier questions an Iraqi man on a rooftop during a nighttime raid at the location of a known terrorist in Mosul, Iraq. Apprehending terrorists is vital for security and stability in Iraq.

Currently, Iraq and Afghanistan are crucial battlegrounds in this war, but the struggle extends far beyond their borders and may well be fought in dozens of other countries simultaneously and for many years to come. Al Qaida and its associated movements operate in more than 80 countries. They have conducted attacks around the world – in New York, Washington, D.C., Jakarta, Bali, Istanbul, Madrid, London, Islamabad, New Delhi, Moscow, Nairobi, Dar Es Salaam, Casablanca, Tunis, Riyadh, Sharm el-Sheikh, and Amman – killing ordinary people of all faiths and ethnicities alike. They exploit poorly governed areas of the world, taking sanctuary where states lack the capacity or the will to police themselves. State sponsors such as Iran and Syria provide yet another form of safe haven. Increasingly, in many states in the developing world, terrorist networks pose a greater threat than external threats.

Victory will come when the enemy's extremist ideologies are discredited in the eyes of their host populations and tacit supporters, becoming unfashionable, and following other discredited creeds, such as Communism and Nazism, into oblivion. This requires the creation of a global environment inhospitable to terrorism. It requires legitimate governments with the capacity to police themselves and to deny terrorists the sanctuary and the resources they need to survive. It also will require support for the establishment of effective representative civil societies around the world, since the appeal of freedom is the best long-term counter to the ideology of the extremists. The ultimate aim is that terrorist networks will no longer have the ability or support to strike globally and catastrophically, and their ability to strike regionally will be outweighed by the capacity and resolve of local governments to defeat them.

Just as these enemies cannot defeat the United States militarily, they cannot be defeated solely through military force. The United States, its allies and partners, will not win this long war in a great battle of annihilation. Victory can only be achieved through the patient accumulation of quiet successes and the orchestration of all elements of national and international power. U.S. military forces are contributing and will continue to contribute to wider government and international efforts to defend the homeland, attack and disrupt terrorist networks, and counter ideological support for terrorism over time. But broad cooperation, across the entire U.S. Government, society, and with NATO, other allies, and partners is essential.

This war is both a battle of arms and a battle of ideas—a fight against terrorist networks and against their murderous ideology. The Department

of Defense fully supports efforts to counter the ideology of terrorism, although most of the U.S. Government's capabilities for this activity reside in other U.S. Government agencies and in the private sector. It is important, however, that the Department continues to improve its ability to understand and engage with key audiences. The Department will work closely with interagency partners to integrate strategic communication into U.S. national security policy planning and operations. The battle of ideas ultimately will be won by enabling moderate Muslim leadership to prevail in their struggle against the violent extremists.

The United States, its allies and partners must maintain the offensive by relentlessly finding, attacking and disrupting terrorist networks worldwide. They must increase global pressure on terrorist networks by denying them sanctuary in both the physical and information domains. They will continue to survey, infiltrate and attack the enemy's global networks and to perturb those networks. Such efforts will yield actionable intelligence that can be operationally exploited with follow-on actions combining military and non-military measures directed against the visible parts of the enemy's network as a means to reach what is hidden. There is, however, no "one size fits all" approach, no "silver bullet." To achieve global effects across countries, regions and groups, the United States must localize and defeat terrorist extremist cells with approaches that are tailored to local conditions and differentiated worldwide. Doing so will help to disaggregate the global network and sever transnational links.

Photo by Technical Sergeant David D. Underwood, Jr., U.S. Air Force.

A Senegalese squad practices maneuvers during small unit training exercises which are part of the Trans - Sahara Counter-Terrorism Initiative (TSCTI), the U.S. Government's long-term interagency plan to combat terrorism in northern Africa.

Long-duration, complex operations involving the U.S. military, other government agencies and international partners will be waged simultaneously in multiple countries around the world, relying on a combination of direct (visible) and indirect (clandestine) approaches. Above all, they will require persistent surveillance and vastly better intelligence to locate enemy capabilities and personnel. They will also require global mobility, rapid strike, sustained unconventional warfare, foreign internal defense, counterterrorism, and counterinsurgency capabilities. Maintaining a long-term, low-visibility presence in many areas of the world where U.S. forces do not traditionally operate will be required. Building and leveraging partner capacity will also be an absolutely essential part of this approach, and the employment of surrogates will be a necessary method for achieving many goals. Working indirectly with and through others, and thereby denying popular support to the enemy, will help to transform the character of the conflict. In many cases, U.S. partners will have greater local knowledge and legitimacy with their own people

and can thereby more effectively fight terrorist networks. Setting security conditions for the expansion of civil society and the rule of law is a related element of this approach.

> "In the absence of…popular support, the mujahed movement would be crushed in the shadows…"
> – Ayman al-Zawahiri, July 2005

Consistent with this approach, defeating terrorist networks highlights the need for the following types of capabilities:

- Human intelligence to discern the intentions of the enemy.

- Persistent surveillance to find and precisely target enemy capabilities in denied areas.

- Capabilities to locate, tag and track terrorists in all domains, including cyberspace.

- Special operations forces to conduct direct action, foreign internal defense, counterterrorist operations and unconventional warfare.

- Multipurpose forces to train, equip, and advise indigenous forces; deploy and engage with partner nations; conduct irregular warfare; and support security, stability, transition, and reconstruction operations.

- Capabilities and organizations to help fuse intelligence and operations to speed action based on time-sensitive intelligence.

- Language and cultural awareness to facilitate the expansion of partner capacity.

- Non-lethal capabilities.

- Urban warfare capabilities.

- Prompt global strike to attack fleeting enemy targets rapidly.

- Riverine warfare capabilities to improve the ability of U.S. forces to work with the security forces of partner countries to deny terrorist groups the use of waterways.

- The ability to communicate U.S. actions effectively to multiple audiences, while rapidly countering enemy agitation and propaganda.

- Joint coordination, procedures, systems and, when necessary, command and control to plan and conduct complex interagency operations.

- Broad, flexible authorities to enable the United States to rapidly develop the capacity of nations to participate effectively in disrupting and defeating terrorist networks.

Defending the Homeland in Depth

Throughout much of its history, the United States enjoyed a geographic position of strategic insularity. The oceans and uncontested borders permitted rapid economic growth and allowed the United States to spend little at home to defend against foreign threats. The advent of long-range bombers and missiles, nuclear weapons, and more recently of terrorist groups with global reach, fundamentally changed the relationship between U.S. geography and security. Geographic insularity no longer confers security for the country.

Globalization enables many positive developments such as the free movement of capital, goods and services, information, people and technology, but it is also accelerating the transmission of disease, the transfer of advanced weapons, the spread of extremist ideologies, the movement of terrorists and the vulnerability of major economic segments. The U.S. populace, territory and infrastructure, as well as its assets in space, may be increasingly vulnerable to these and a variety of other threats, including weapons of mass destruction, missile and other air threats, and electronic or cyber-attacks.

Globalization also empowers small groups and individuals. Nation-states no longer have a monopoly over the catastrophic use of violence. Today, small teams or even single individuals can weaponize chemical, biological and even crude radiological or nuclear devices and use them to murder hundreds of thousands of people. Loosely organized and with few assets of their own to protect, non-state enemies are considerably more difficult than nation-states to deter through traditional military means. Non-state enemies could attempt to attack a wide range of targets including government facilities; commercial and financial systems; cultural and historical landmarks; food, water, and power supplies; and information, transport, and energy networks. They will employ unconventional means to penetrate homeland defenses and exploit the very nature of western societies – their openness – to attack their citizens, economic institutions, physical infrastructure and social fabric.

"The need [is] to inflict the maximum casualties against the opponent, for this is the language understood by the west, no matter how much time and effort such operations take."
– Ayman al-Zawahiri, 2001.

The threat to the U.S. homeland, however, is broader than that posed by terrorists. Hostile states could also attack the United States using WMD delivered by missiles or by less familiar means such as commercial shipping or general aviation. They could attack surreptitiously through surrogates. Some hostile states are pursuing advanced weapons of mass destruction, including genetically engineered biological warfare agents that can overcome today's defenses. There is also a danger that the WMD capabilities of some states could fall into the hands of, or be given to, terrorists who could use them to attack the United States.

As set forth in the Defense Department's *National Maritime Security Policy* and in the *Strategy for Homeland Defense and Civil Support*, the Department's strategic goal for homeland defense is to secure the United States from direct attack. To achieve this goal, the Department will work as part of an interagency effort, with the Department of Homeland Security and other Federal, state and local agencies, to address threats to the U.S. homeland. The Department will maintain a deterrent posture to persuade potential aggressors that their objectives in attacking would be denied and that any attack on U.S. territory, people, critical infrastructure (including through cyberspace) or forces could result in an overwhelming response. U.S. forces must be capable of defeating threats at a distance and of swiftly mitigating the consequences of an attack. Capabilities to mitigate attacks on the U.S. homeland may also play a role in responding to natural disasters, as the response to Hurricane Katrina demonstrated. Over time, the goal is that the capacity of other agencies and state and local governments to respond to domestic incidents will be sufficient to perform their assigned responsibilities with minimal reliance on U.S. military support. To that end, the Department will develop concepts of operations to leverage its strengths in areas such as planning, training and command and control, in support of its interagency homeland security partners.

A National Guard multi-purpose utility truck fords Hurricane Katrina floodwaters to bring supplies to victims in downtown New Orleans, Louisiana.

Protecting the U.S. homeland requires an active and layered defense strategy. The strategy emphasizes partnerships with neighboring states and allies, as well as with other Federal, state and local agencies. The Department's *Strategy for Homeland Defense and Civil Support* identifies three different roles it plays: <u>leading</u> Department-specific assigned missions; <u>supporting</u> other agencies; and helping to <u>enable</u> partners.

<u>Lead</u>. At the direction of the President or the Secretary of Defense, the Department of Defense executes military missions that dissuade, deter or defeat external attacks upon the United States, its population, and its defense critical infrastructure.

The Department plays an important role in identifying and characterizing threats at the earliest possible time so that, where possible, they can be prevented, disrupted, interdicted, or otherwise defeated. In the air domain, the Department has primary responsibility for defending U.S. airspace and protecting the nation's air approaches. In the maritime approaches, the Department works alongside the Department of Homeland Security to integrate U.S. maritime defense – optimizing the mutually supporting capabilities of the U.S. Navy and the U.S. Coast Guard. Forward deployed naval assets work with other agencies to identify, track, and intercept threats before they threaten the United States. The Department remains prepared to reinforce the defense of the land approaches to the United States if directed by the President.

Through its deterrent force posture and capabilities, the Department seeks to convince adversaries that they cannot achieve their objectives through attacks on the U.S. homeland, and that any attack will prompt a swift response. U.S. forces are prepared to: intercept and defeat threats against U.S. territory, within U.S. territorial waters and airspace, and at a distance from the homeland; protect against and mitigate the consequences of any attack; and / or conduct military operations in response to any attack. The

Department has begun deploying interceptors to protect the U.S. homeland from ballistic missile attack. It is taking steps to ensure it can continue to perform its assigned duties during or after an attack. It ensures the nation's ability to respond to an attack by protecting its forces and the defense-critical infrastructure necessary to project power and sustain operations.

<u>Support</u>. At the direction of the President or Secretary of Defense, the Department supports civil authorities for designated law enforcement and / or other activities and as part of a comprehensive national response to prevent and protect against terrorist incidents or to recover from an attack or a disaster. As discussed, the Department's substantial humanitarian contributions to relief efforts in the aftermaths of Hurricanes Katrina and Rita fall into this category. In the future, should other catastrophes overwhelm civilian capacity, the Department may be called upon to respond rapidly with additional resources as part of an overall U.S. Government effort. In order to respond effectively to future catastrophic events, the Department will provide U.S. NORTHCOM with authority to stage forces and equipment domestically prior to potential incidents when possible. The Department will also seek to eliminate current legislative ceilings on pre-event spending.

<u>Enable</u>. The Department seeks to improve the homeland defense and consequence management capabilities of its national and international partners and to improve the Department's capabilities by sharing information, expertise and technology as appropriate across military

and civilian boundaries. The Department does this by leveraging its comparative advantages in planning, training, command and control and exercising and by developing trust and confidence through shared training and exercises. Successful homeland defense requires standardizing operational concepts, developing compatible technology solutions and coordinating planning. Toward that end, the Department will work with the Department of Homeland Security and with state and local governments to improve homeland security capabilities and cooperation. Working together will improve interagency planning and scenario development and enhance interoperability through experimentation, testing and training exercises.

Overall, consistent with the *National Maritime Security Policy* and the *Strategy for Homeland Defense and Civil Support*, defending the homeland in depth and mitigating the consequences of attacks highlight the need for the following types of capabilities:

- Joint command and control for homeland defense and civil support missions, including communications and command and control systems that are interoperable with other agencies and state and local governments.

- Air and maritime domain awareness capabilities to provide increased situational awareness and shared information on potential threats through rapid collection, fusion and analysis.

- Capabilities to manage the consequences of major catastrophic events.

U.S. Navy Search and Rescue personnel retrieve an evacuee victim of Hurricane Katrina from a rooftop in New Orleans, Louisiana. The Navy's involvement in the humanitarian assistance operations is led by the Federal Emergency Management Agency (FEMA), in conjunction with the Department of Defense.

Photo by Photographer's Mate 3rd Class Jay C. Pugh, U.S. Navy.

- Broad spectrum medical countermeasures to defend against genetically engineered or naturally mutating pathogens for which there are no current defenses.

- Tailored deterrence, including prompt global strike capabilities to defend and respond in an overwhelming manner against WMD attacks, and air and missile defenses, as well as other defensive measures, to deter attacks by demonstrating the ability to deny an adversary's objectives.

- New or expanded authorities to improve access to Guard and reserve forces for use in the event of a man-made or natural disaster.

Shaping the Choices of Countries at Strategic Crossroads

The choices that major and emerging powers make will affect the future strategic position and freedom of action of the United States, its allies and partners. The United States will attempt to shape these choices in ways that foster cooperation and mutual security interests. At the same time, the United States, its allies and partners must also hedge against the possibility that a major or emerging power could choose a hostile path in the future. The pursuit of exclusionary or coercive policies and the development of high-end military capabilities that target U.S. or coalition forces are of particular concern.

Beyond Europe and the Asia-Pacific region, the Middle East, Central Asia and Latin America are in flux and represent new geo-strategic crossroads. The United States will seek to shape not only the choices of countries in those regions, but choices of countries outside them that have interests or ambitions within them.

Many countries in the Middle East find themselves at strategic crossroads. Democracy is emerging in Iraq, giving political voice to people who suffered for decades under a ruthless tyranny. Freedom is also taking root in Lebanon. Libya has decided to give up its nuclear program. Many countries in the region are acting in partnership with the United States to combat terrorist networks. Although positive developments have been made, the region remains volatile. Many states continue to face internal security threats. The pursuit of weapons of mass destruction by Iran is a destabilizing factor in the region. Terrorist networks remain active in many states and could threaten regional energy supplies in an attempt to cripple the global economy.

The countries of Central Asia have emerged from decades of Communist rule, but some countries still have a long way to go toward adopting basic political liberties and free markets. States in the region face the threat of Islamist terrorist extremism. The energy resources of the region offer both an opportunity for economic development, as well as a danger that outside powers may seek to gain influence over those resources.

In Latin America, there has been steady progress toward political and economic development over the past several decades. Still, slow economic growth, weak democratic institutions and continuing stark economic inequality have led to a resurgence of populist authoritarian political movements in some countries, such as Venezuela. These movements threaten the gains achieved and are a source of political and economic instability.

Beyond these regions, the choices of major and emerging powers, including India, Russia and China, will be key factors in determining the international security environment of the 21st century.

India is emerging as a great power and a key strategic partner. On July 18, 2005 the President and Indian Prime Minister declared their resolve to transform the U.S.-India relationship into a global partnership that will provide leadership in areas of mutual concern and interest. Shared values as long-standing, multi-ethnic democracies provide the foundation for continued and increased strategic cooperation and represent an important opportunity for our two countries.

Russia remains a country in transition. It is

unlikely to pose a military threat to the United States or its allies on the same scale or intensity as the Soviet Union during the Cold War. Where possible, the United States will cooperate with Russia on shared interests such as countering the proliferation of weapons of mass destruction, combating terrorism, and countering the trafficking of narcotics. The United States remains concerned about the erosion of democracy in Russia, the curtailment of non-governmental organizations (NGOs) and freedom of the press, the centralization of political power and limits on economic freedom. Internationally, the United States welcomes Russia as a constructive partner but views with increasing concern its sales of disruptive weapons technologies abroad and actions that compromise the political and economic independence and territorial integrity of other states.

Of the major and emerging powers, China has the greatest potential to compete militarily with the United States and field disruptive military technologies that could over time offset traditional U.S. military advantages absent U.S. counter strategies. U.S. policy remains focused on encouraging China to play a constructive, peaceful role in the Asia-Pacific region and to serve as a partner in addressing common security challenges, including terrorism, proliferation, narcotics and piracy. U.S. policy seeks to encourage China to choose a path of peaceful economic growth and political liberalization, rather than military threat and intimidation. The United States' goal is for China to continue as an economic partner and emerge as a responsible stakeholder and force for good in the world.

A Tomahawk Land Attack Missile is launched from the USS Florida during Giant Shadow, a U.S. Navy experimental exercise. The USS Florida is one of four nuclear ballistic missile submarines being converted to conventional-warhead guided missile submarines. After conversion, the submarines will be able to launch Tomahawk Missiles, Unmanned Underwater and Aerial Vehicles and Special Forces personnel and equipment.

China continues to invest heavily in its military, particularly in its strategic arsenal and capabilities designed to improve its ability to project power beyond its borders. Since 1996, China has increased its defense spending by more than 10% in real terms in every year except 2003. Secrecy, moreover, envelops most aspects of Chinese security affairs. The outside world has little knowledge of Chinese motivations and decision-making or of key capabilities supporting its military modernization. The United States encourages China to take actions to make its intentions clear and clarify its military plans.

Chinese military modernization has accelerated since the mid-to-late 1990s in response to central leadership demands to develop military options against Taiwan scenarios. The pace and scope of China's military build-up already puts regional military balances at risk. China is likely to continue making large investments in high-end, asymmetric military capabilities, emphasizing electronic and cyber-warfare; counter-space operations; ballistic and cruise missiles; advanced integrated air defense systems; next generation torpedoes; advanced submarines; strategic nuclear strike from modern, sophisticated land- and sea-based systems; and theater unmanned aerial vehicles for employment by the Chinese military and for global export. These capabilities, the vast distances of the Asian theater, China's continental depth, and the challenge of en route and in-theater U.S. basing place a premium on forces capable of sustained operations at great distances into denied areas.

The United States will work to ensure that all major and emerging powers are integrated as constructive actors and stakeholders into the international system. It will also seek to ensure that no foreign power can dictate the terms of regional or global security. It will attempt to dissuade any military competitor from developing disruptive or other capabilities that could enable regional hegemony or hostile action against the United States or other friendly countries, and it will seek to deter aggression or coercion. Should deterrence fail, the United States would deny a hostile power its strategic and operational objectives.

Shaping the choices of major and emerging powers requires a balanced approach, one that seeks cooperation but also creates prudent hedges against the possibility that cooperative approaches by themselves may fail to preclude future conflict. A successful hedging strategy requires improving the capacity of partner states and reducing their vulnerabilities. In this regard, the United States will work to achieve greater integration of defensive systems among its international partners in ways that would complicate any adversary's efforts to decouple them. The United States will work with allies and partners to integrate intelligence sensors, communication networks, information systems, missile defenses, undersea warfare and counter-mine warfare capabilities. It will seek to strengthen partner nations' capabilities to defend themselves and withstand attack, including against ambiguous coercive threats.

An F-15 Eagle pilot assigned as an exchange officer to Nyutabaru Air Base, Japan (right) discusses tactics with a Japan Air Self Defense Force F-15 pilot (left) before a mission. The U.S. alliance with Japan is important to the stability in the Asia-Pacific region.

To dissuade major and emerging powers from developing capabilities that could threaten regional stability, to deter conflict, and to defeat aggression should deterrence fail, the United States is further diversifying its basing posture. Based on the Department's Global Defense Posture Review, the United States will continue to adapt its global posture to promote constructive bilateral relations, mitigate anti-access threats and offset potential political coercion designed to limit U.S. access to any region. The United States will develop capabilities that would present any adversary with complex and multidimensional challenges and complicate its offensive planning efforts. These include the pursuit of investments that capitalize on enduring U.S. advantages in key strategic and operational areas, such as persistent surveillance and long-range strike, stealth, operational maneuver and sustainment of air, sea and ground forces at strategic distances, air dominance and undersea warfare. These capabilities should preserve U.S. freedom of action and provide future Presidents with an expanded set of options to address all of the QDR focus areas and a wide range of potential future contingencies. The aim is to possess sufficient capability to convince any potential adversary that it cannot prevail in a conflict and that engaging in conflict entails substantial strategic risks beyond military defeat.

Consistent with this approach, shaping the choices of countries at strategic crossroads highlights the need for the following types of capabilities:

- Security cooperation and engagement activities including joint training exercises, senior staff talks, and officer and foreign internal

U.S. Air National Guard personnel familiarize their Polish counterparts with aspects of the F-16 Fighting Falcon during the U.S. European Command exercise Sentry White Falcon 2005. In 2006, the Polish Air Force will begin receiving delivery of 48 F-16 Fighting Falcons they purchased to begin replacing their Soviet-made MiG fighters as the country modernizes its military to NATO standards.

defense training to increase understanding, strengthen allies and partners, and accurately communicate U.S. objectives and intent. This will require both new authorities and 21st century mechanisms for the interagency process.

- Considerably improved language and cultural awareness to develop a greater understanding of emerging powers and how they may approach strategic choices.

- Persistent surveillance, including systems that can penetrate and loiter in denied or contested areas.

- The capability to deploy rapidly, assemble, command, project, reconstitute, and re-employ joint combat power from all domains to facilitate assured access.

- Prompt and high-volume global strike to deter aggression or coercion, and if deterrence fails, to provide a broader range of conventional response options to the President. This will require broader authorities from the Congress.

- Secure broadband communications into denied or contested areas to support penetrating surveillance and strike systems.

- Integrated defenses against short-, intermediate-, and intercontinental-range ballistic and cruise missile systems.

- Air dominance capabilities to defeat advanced threats.

- Undersea warfare capabilities to exploit stealth

and enhance deterrence.

- Capabilities to shape and defend cyberspace.

- Joint command and control capabilities that are survivable in the face of WMD-, electronic-, or cyber-attacks.

Preventing the Acquisition or Use of Weapons of Mass Destruction

During the Cold War, the main challenge facing the United States was deterring the former Soviet Union from using weapons of mass destruction (WMD) against the United States and its allies. Today, the United States faces a greater danger from an expanding number of hostile regimes and terrorist groups that seek to acquire and use WMD. These actors may not respond to traditional tools and concepts of deterrence.

A number of potentially hostile states possess or seek weapons of mass destruction. For these states, WMD – particularly nuclear weapons – provide the means to assert regional hegemony and intimidate others. They may brandish nuclear, chemical and biological weapons to ensure regime survival, deny the United States access to critical areas, or deter others from taking action against them. Even when they do not pose a direct military threat to the United States, these states may threaten the United States or its allies indirectly by transferring weapons or expertise to terrorists. North Korea has pursued nuclear, chemical and biological weapons and has developed and sold weapons, including long-range missiles, to other states of concern.

Iran's pursuit of nuclear capabilities, support for terrorism, and threatening statements about regional neighbors raise similar concerns about its intentions. Iran is rapidly developing long-range delivery systems and a full nuclear fuel cycle that would enable it to produce nuclear weapons.

> *"Israel must be wiped off the map. And God willing, with the force of God behind it, we shall soon experience a world without the United States and Zionism." Iranian President Ahmadinejad, October 2005*

In the event of a conflict, WMD-armed states could use their weapons against the United States or its allies preemptively, during conflict or to slow follow-on stabilization efforts. In some cases, states could have hundreds of suspect facilities and storage sites that would need to be secured, searched and remediated following the end of combat. Such operations could overwhelm stabilization efforts.

Several other WMD-armed states, although not necessarily hostile to the United States, could face the possibility of internal instability and loss of control over their weapons. The lack of effective governance in many parts of the world contributes to the WMD danger, providing opportunities for terrorist organizations to acquire or harbor WMD. The prospect that a nuclear-capable state may lose control of some of its weapons to terrorists is one of the greatest dangers the United States and its allies face.

Technological trends heighten the threat. Nuclear weapons, sophisticated and/or bio-engineered biological agents, and non-traditional chemical agents – once the sole purview of large, complex state weapons programs – will be within reach of a growing number of actors in the coming decades. Technological advances and widely distributed technical information are making ever more dangerous weapons easier to produce. At the same time, expanded reliance on sophisticated electronic technologies by the United States, its allies and partners increases their vulnerability to the destructive effects of electromagnetic pulse (EMP) – the energy burst given off during a nuclear weapon explosion. The effect of a nuclear blast could be catastrophic to both military forces and the civilian population.

It is extremely difficult to collect reliable intelligence on WMD programs and activities, which are closely guarded secrets. The prevalence of dual-use technologies and legitimate civilian applications means nuclear, chemical and biological research efforts are easy to conceal and difficult to detect and monitor. Based on the demonstrated ease with which uncooperative states and non-state actors can conceal WMD programs and related activities, the United States, its allies and partners must expect further intelligence gaps and surprises.

It is in this environment that terrorists – including Osama bin Laden and his associates – seek to acquire these catastrophic weapons and technologies, preying on vulnerable governments, ungoverned territories and susceptible individuals. They benefit from determined proliferators and criminal enterprises that seek to traffic in catastrophic technologies and that continue to aid and abet them.

> *Posted Monday, January 11, 1999*
>
> *TIME Reporter: "The U.S. says you are trying to acquire chemical and nuclear weapons."*
>
> *Osama bin Laden: "Acquiring weapons for the defense of Muslims is a religious duty. If I have indeed acquired these weapons, then I thank God for enabling me to do so. And if I seek to acquire these weapons, I am carrying out a duty. It would be a sin for Muslims not to try to possess the weapons that would prevent the infidels from inflicting harm on Muslims."*

The principal objective of the United States is to prevent hostile states or non-state actors from acquiring WMD. This involves diplomatic and economic measures, but it can also involve active measures and the use of military force to deny access to materials, interdict transfers, and disrupt production programs. For example, in October 2003, German and Italian authorities, acting under the framework of the Proliferation Security Initiative (PSI) and based on information provided by the United States, stopped a shipment of advanced centrifuge parts bound for Libya's nuclear program. Two months after confronting Libyan officials with this new evidence of an active and illegal nuclear program, Libya voluntarily agreed to end its WMD and long-range missile programs. Yet despite such successes, additional states and some terrorist organizations may nevertheless acquire WMD in the coming years.

To address such threats, the United States must be prepared to deter attacks; locate, tag and track WMD materials; act in cases where a state that possesses WMD loses control of its weapons, especially nuclear devices; detect WMD across all domains; sustain operations even while under WMD attack; help mitigate the consequences of WMD attacks at home or overseas; and eliminate WMD materials in peacetime, during combat, and after conflicts. National efforts to counter the threat posed by weapons of mass destruction must incorporate both preventive and responsive dimensions.

Preventive Dimension: The United States seeks to build and expand global partnerships aimed at preventing proliferation; stopping WMD-related trafficking; helping friendly governments improve controls over existing weapons, materials and expertise; and discrediting weapons of mass destruction as instruments of national power. Improving the ability to detect, identify, locate, tag and track key WMD assets and development infrastructure in hostile or denied areas and to interdict WMD, their delivery systems, and related materials in transit are essential to this approach. In addition, the United States must improve its ability to identify and penetrate criminal networks bent on profiting from the proliferation of such dangerous weapons and

Photo by Photographer's Mate 2nd Class Aaron Peterson, U.S. Navy.

U.S. and Pakistani sailors prepare to conduct boardings in a simulated maritime interdiction operation. In 2003, international cooperation led to the interdiction of a shipment of centrifuge parts to Libya. This action, combined with Pakistani arrests of A.Q. Khan network affiliates, helped to successfully shut down the sophisticated black market network.

expertise. Multinational efforts such as PSI provide a model to expand global cooperation to prevent proliferation.

Responsive Dimension: If prevention efforts fail, the United States must be prepared to respond. An effective response requires that the United States use all elements of national power, working with like-minded nations, to locate, secure, and destroy WMD. The United States will use peaceful and cooperative means whenever possible, but will employ force when necessary. This will require growing emphasis on WMD elimination operations that locate, characterize, secure, disable and/or destroy a state or non-state actor's WMD capabilities and programs in a hostile or uncertain environment. The Military Departments will organize, train and equip joint forces for this increasingly important mission.

There are two particularly difficult operational and technical challenges associated with WMD elimination: detecting fissile material and rendering safe nuclear, chemical and biological devices. This requires the ability to locate, tag and track fissile materials rapidly, including in denied areas, and to deploy specialized teams trained to render safe nuclear weapons quickly anywhere in the world.

Finally, if a WMD attack cannot be prevented, the Department must be prepared to respond to requests to help mitigate the effects of the attack at the earliest opportunity, initiate or support ongoing consequence management efforts, and actively support local, state, Federal and allied and partner authorities. To ensure that its responses to the new WMD threat are considered both credible and legitimate, the United States will work closely with its partners, allies, and other members of the international community.

Consistent with this approach, preventing state or non-state actors from acquiring or using WMD highlights the need for the following types of capabilities:

- Special operations forces to locate, characterize and secure WMD.

- Capabilities to locate, tag and track WMD, their delivery systems and related materials, including the means to move such items.

- Capabilities to detect fissile materials such as nuclear devices at stand-off ranges.

- Interdiction capabilities to stop air, maritime, and ground shipments of WMD, their delivery systems and related materials.

- Persistent surveillance over wide areas to locate WMD capabilities or hostile forces.

- Human intelligence, language skills and cultural awareness to understand better the intentions and motivations of potential adversaries and to speed recovery efforts.

- Capabilities and specialized teams to render safe and secure WMD.

- Non-lethal weapons to secure WMD sites so that materials cannot be removed.

- Joint command and control tailored for the

WMD elimination mission.

- The capability to deploy, sustain, protect, support and re-deploy special operations forces in hostile environments.

- The capability to shield critical and vulnerable systems and technologies from the catastrophic effects of EMP.

A U.S. Navy Hospital Corpsman (left) and Department of Defense Civilian Equipment Specialist (right) discuss assembling a Chemical Biological Protective Shelter during a training session at Camp Coyote, Kuwait. The Department leverages expertise in all elements of the Total Force to conduct operations.

Refining the Department's Force Planning Construct for Wartime

The four focus areas informed the Department's review of the guidance for sizing and shaping the U.S. Armed Forces. This guidance is commonly referred to as the Department's Force Planning Construct. Such guidance informs the analysis that provides a guide to determine both the appropriate size of the force (capacity), as well as the types of capabilities (forces and equipment) needed across a range of scenarios.

The 2001 QDR led the Department to direct the military to organize, train and equip sufficient forces to defend the U.S. homeland; operate in and from four forward regions; "swiftly defeat" adversaries in two overlapping military campaigns while preserving for the President the option to "win decisively" one of those campaigns; and conduct a limited number of lesser military and humanitarian contingencies.

During this QDR, senior leaders confirmed the importance of the main elements of that Force Planning Construct: maintaining the ability to defend the U.S. homeland; continuing to operate in and from forward areas; and above all, the importance of maintaining capabilities and forces to wage multiple campaigns in an overlapping time frame – for which there may be little or no warning of attack. This latter capability in particular remains a strong deterrent against opportunistic aggression or attempted coercion. At the same time, lessons learned from recent operations suggest the need for some refinement of the construct to take better account of wartime demands:

- The Department's homeland defense responsibilities should be more clearly distinguished from the responsibilities of other agencies.

- U.S. forces must continue to operate in forward areas, but operational demands over the past four years demonstrate the need to operate around the globe and not only in and from the four regions called out in the 2001 QDR (Europe, the Middle East, the Asian Littoral, and Northeast Asia).

- In the post-September 11 world, irregular warfare has emerged as the dominant form of warfare confronting the United States, its allies and its partners; accordingly, guidance must account for distributed, long-duration operations, including unconventional warfare, foreign internal defense, counterterrorism, counterinsurgency, and stabilization and reconstruction operations.

- For the foreseeable future, steady-state operations, including operations as part of a long war against terrorist networks, and associated rotation base and sustainment requirements, will be the main determinant for sizing U.S. forces.

- Consistent with the QDR's emphasis on prevention, guidance must place greater emphasis on forces and capabilities needed for deterrence and other peacetime shaping activities.

- Finally, operational end-states defined in terms of "swiftly defeating" or "winning decisively" against adversaries may be less useful for some types of operations U.S. forces may be directed to conduct, such as supporting civil authorities to manage the consequences of catastrophic, mass casualty events at home, or conducting a long-duration, irregular warfare campaign against enemies employing asymmetric tactics.

Based on these considerations, the Department has refined its Force Planning Construct, dividing its activities into three objective areas: Homeland Defense, War on Terror / Irregular (Asymmetric) Warfare and Conventional Campaigns. In

U.S. military forces are deployed around the globe conducting operations in accordance with the Force Planning Construct refined for wartime. The amphibious assault ship USS Iwo Jima sits pierside in New Orleans, Louisiana, in support of Hurricane Katrina humanitarian assistance operations. U.S. Army soldiers and U.S. Marines look for weapons caches and insurgents near the Syrian border in Iraq. A B-2 Spirit bomber soars during a deployment to Andersen Air Force Base, Guam, as part of a rotation that has provided U.S. Pacific Command a continuous bomber presence in the Asia-Pacific region. (photos top to bottom)

all cases, the Department should increase its capabilities to conduct operations against enemies who employ asymmetric approaches. This refined Force Planning Construct for wartime describes the relative level of effort the Department should devote to each of the three objective areas. In

each area, it accounts both for activities that the Department conducts continuously (steady-state) as well as those it conducts episodically (surge). In addition to normal force generation, sustainment and training activities, this wartime force planning construct calls for U.S. forces to be able to:

Defend the Homeland

- <u>Steady-state</u> – detect, deter, and if necessary, defeat external threats to the U.S. homeland, and enable partners to contribute to U.S. national security. Examples of such activities include: routine homeland security training and exercises with other Federal agencies and state and local governments; strategic deterrence; routine maritime operations conducted with the U.S. Coast Guard; North American air defense, including air sovereignty operations; missile defense; and readiness to provide support to civil authorities for consequence management events.

- <u>Surge</u> – contribute to the nation's response to and management of the consequences of WMD attacks or a catastrophic event, such as Hurricane Katrina, and also to raise the level of defense responsiveness in all domains (e.g., air, land, maritime, space and cyberspace) if directed.

<u>Prevail</u> in the <u>War on Terror and Conduct Irregular Operations</u>

- <u>Steady-state</u> – deter and defend against external transnational terrorist attacks, enable partners through integrated security cooperation programs, and conduct multiple, globally distributed irregular operations of varying duration. Employ general purpose forces continuously to interact with allies, build partner capability, conduct long-duration counter insurgency operations and deter aggressors through forward presence.

- Surge – conduct a large-scale, potentially long-duration irregular warfare campaign including counterinsurgency and security, stability, transition and reconstruction operations. An example of an irregular surge campaign would be the current level of effort associated with operations in Iraq and Afghanistan.

Conduct and Win Conventional Campaigns

- Steady-state – deter inter-state coercion or aggression through forward deployed forces, enable partners through theater security cooperation, and conduct presence missions. These activities include day-to-day presence missions, military-to-military exchanges, combined exercises, security cooperation activities and normal increases in readiness during the seasonal exercises of potential adversaries.

- Surge – wage two nearly simultaneous conventional campaigns (or one conventional campaign if already engaged in a large-scale, long-duration irregular campaign), while selectively reinforcing deterrence against opportunistic acts of aggression. Be prepared in one of the two campaigns to remove a hostile regime, destroy its military capacity and set conditions for the transition to, or for the restoration of, civil society.

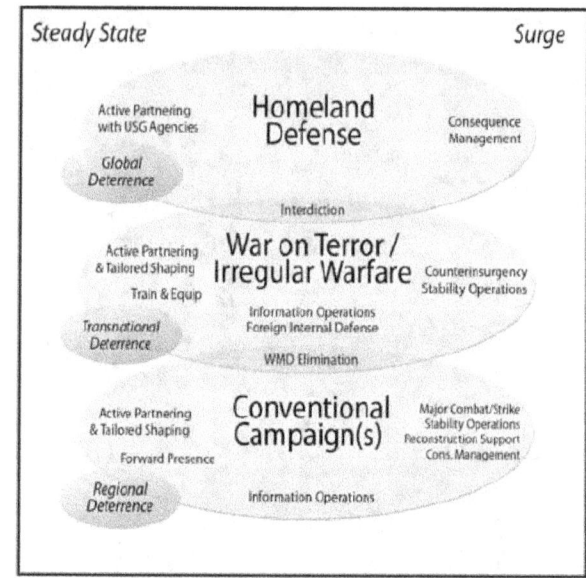

This refined force planning construct for wartime will be used in lieu of the force planning guidance published in the March 2005 *National Defense Strategy*. The Department will use this construct as the basis for future analysis of needed capabilities and forces.

In conducting follow-on analyses and assessments to determine more fully the implications of this guidance, U.S. operational and force planning will consider a somewhat higher level of contributions from international allies and partners, as well as other Federal agencies, in surge operations ranging from homeland defense to irregular warfare and conventional campaigns. This assumption is consistent with the increased level of security cooperation and other activities to enable partners as required by the refined Force Planning Construct. The construct also acknowledges that policy decisions, such as mobilization policies and war aims, may change over time and have implications for the shape and size of U.S. forces. Finally, as part of a process of continuous reassessment and improvement, this wartime construct will be further developed over time to differentiate among the Military Departments as to how they should best size and shape their unique force structures, for use by the Combatant Commanders, since all parts of the construct do not apply equally to all capability portfolios.

REORIENTING CAPABILITIES AND FORCES

During the QDR, the senior leadership of the Department considered potential adjustments to capabilities and forces in light of the four focus areas and refined Force Planning Construct. They identified desired future force characteristics prior to developing proposals for the following capability portfolios: joint ground; special operations forces; joint air; joint maritime; tailored deterrence; combating WMD; joint mobility; ISR and space capabilities; net-centricity; and joint command and control. As part of a process of continuous change, the Department's capabilities and forces will be reoriented over time to reflect these desired characteristics.

This reorientation builds upon transformational changes already underway, shifting the joint force: from dependence on large, permanent overseas garrisons toward expeditionary operations utilizing more austere bases abroad; from focusing primarily on traditional combat operations toward greater capability to deal with asymmetric challenges; from deconflicting joint operations to integrated and even interdependent operations – all while massing the cumulative power of joint forces to achieve synergistic effects.

Insights derived from a series of complementary analyses, including the Mobility Capabilities Study and the Joint Staff's Operational Availability (OA) Studies, informed capability portfolio development. The Operational Availability series

of studies is a four-year ongoing joint analytical effort to assess force capabilities and capacities to meet the priorities of the *National Defense Strategy*. These analyses helped to identify the Department's progress in each capability portfolio since 2001, gaps in capabilities needed to realize the future force vision, insights about potential excess capacity, and future opportunities for investment. For example, Operational Availability assessed the availability of forces prior to, during and following major combat operations, as well as to meet routine missions and the increased demands of the long war. It revealed shortfalls in capabilities for special operations forces and intelligence, surveillance and reconnaissance, among other capabilities.

Based on the Operational Availability analysis, other related assessments, and extensive senior leader discussions, the Department concluded that the size of today's forces – both the Active and Reserve Components across the Military Departments – is appropriate to meet current and projected operational demands. At the same time, these analyses highlighted the need to continue re-balancing the mix of joint capabilities and forces. This chapter summarizes recommended changes in the mix of capabilities and the Department's resource priorities. The President's Budget for Fiscal Year 2007 reflects the QDR's "leading edge" priorities to change the mix of capabilities in key areas. The full budgetary and programmatic implications of the QDR will be reflected in the upcoming budget cycle.

Joint Ground Forces

Vision. Joint ground forces will continue to take on more of the tasks performed by today's special operations forces. The result will be a new breed of warrior able to move more easily between disparate mission sets while preserving their depth of skill in primary specialties. Future warriors will be as proficient in irregular operations, including counterinsurgency and stabilization operations, as they are today in high-intensity combat. They will be modular in structure at all levels, largely self-sustaining, and capable of operating both in traditional formations as well as disaggregating into smaller, autonomous units. They will be able to sustain long-duration irregular operations, while exploiting reach-back to non-deployed elements of the force. They will understand foreign cultures and societies and possess the ability to train, mentor and advise foreign security forces and conduct counterinsurgency campaigns. They will have increased capabilities to conduct time-sensitive operations, by fusing intelligence and operations at the tactical level and with larger numbers of Joint Tactical Air Controllers to achieve a higher level of joint ground-air integration.

Progress to Date. Consistent with these future force characteristics, the Army is significantly expanding its capabilities and capacity for the full range of military operations, including irregular warfare and support to security, stability and transition operations. It is reorganizing its combat and support forces into modular brigade-based units – including brigade combat teams (BCTs) and the support brigades to sustain them – to increase breadth and depth for the long war. They are increasing their proficiency in irregular warfare, thereby freeing up some special operations forces for more complex tasks. Tactical and operational headquarters have been redesigned to support geographically distributed brigade operations and provide joint command and control. In 2004, the Army terminated the Comanche helicopter program and reallocated funds to reinvigorate its aviation capabilities, including unmanned aerial vehicles. The restructured Future Combat Systems (FCS) program is accelerating "spin-outs" of advanced capabilities into the new Army modular forces, as well as for U.S. SOCOM and the Marine Corps.

The Marine Corps has increased both its capacity and its capability to conduct irregular warfare. Since 2001, the Marines Corps has realigned its force structure to address lessons learned in recent operations, resulting in a 12% increase in infantry capacity and related intelligence support to infantry units, an additional Active Component rotary wing aircraft squadron, a 25% increase in light armor units, a 38% increase in reconnaissance capacity, 50% more Joint Fire Liaison Teams and a 30% increase in reserve intelligence structure. It has also established Foreign Military Training

Photo by Staff Sergeant James L. Harper Jr., U.S. Air Force.

U.S. Army soldiers conduct a patrol in Mosul, Iraq, in support of Operation Iraqi Freedom. Their Stryker vehicles enable them to maneuver rapidly in both urban environments and open terrain.

Units to train indigenous forces worldwide. This rebalancing has increased potential Marine Corps contributions, especially for preventive actions and irregular warfare operations. Additionally, the Marine Corps has increased the capability of the individual Marine to conduct distributed operations, providing the Combatant Commanders an expeditionary force able to conduct "low-end" SOF missions as well as traditional operations.

QDR Decisions. To achieve future joint ground force characteristics and build on progress to date, the Department will:

- Continue to rebalance capabilities by creating modular brigades in all three Army components: 117 in the Regular Army (42 BCTs and 75 support brigades); 106 in the Army National Guard (28 BCTs and 78 support brigades); and 58 support brigades in the U.S. Army Reserve. This equates to a 46 percent increase in readily available combat power and a better balance between combat and support forces.

- Transform Army units and headquarters to modular designs.

- Incorporate FCS improvements into the modular force through a spiral development effort that will introduce new technologies as they are developed.

- Expand the Air Force Joint Tactical Air Control program by jointly training personnel for air/ground operations and use of Unmanned Aerial Vehicles.

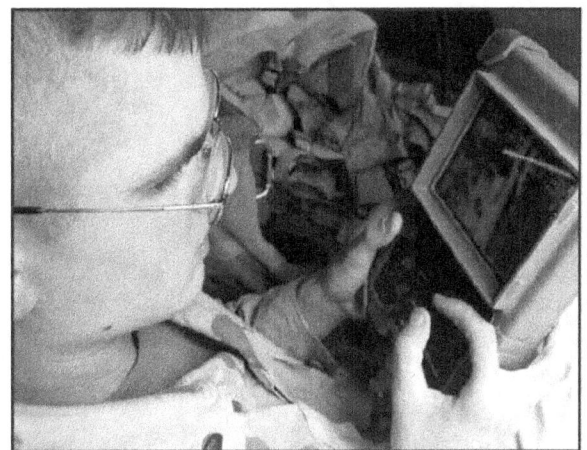

The small, tactical Raven unmanned aerial vehicle is an example of UAVs being employed by ground forces to provide persistent, remote surveillance and reconnaissance for U.S. forces beyond their line of sight. This Raven pictured at bottom is used to identify and deter the placement of improvised explosive devices on Route Trans-Am, Iraq.

- Stabilize the Army's end strength at 482,400 Active and 533,000 Reserve Component personnel by Fiscal Year 2011.

- Stabilize the Marine Corps' end strength at 175,000 Active and 39,000 Reserve Component personnel by Fiscal Year 2011.

Special Operations Forces (SOF)

Vision. The future special operations force will be rapidly deployable, agile, flexible and tailorable to perform the most demanding and sensitive missions worldwide. As general purpose joint ground forces take on tasks that Special Operations Forces (SOF) currently perform, SOF will increase their capacity to perform more demanding and specialized tasks, especially long-duration, indirect and clandestine operations in politically sensitive environments and denied areas. For direct action, they will possess an expanded organic ability to locate, tag and track dangerous individuals and other high-value targets globally. SOF will also have greater capacity to detect, locate and render safe WMD. For unconventional warfare and training foreign forces, future SOF will have the capacity to operate in dozens of countries simultaneously. SOF will have increased ability to train and work with partners, employ surrogates, operate clandestinely and sustain a larger posture with lower visibility. SOF will sustain current language and cultural skills while increasing regional proficiency specific to key geographic operational areas: the Middle East, Asia, Africa and Latin America. Longer duration operations will emphasize building personal relationships with foreign military and security forces and other indigenous assets to achieve common objectives.

<u>Progress to Date</u>. There have been impressive gains in SOF capabilities since 2001, supported by an 81% increase in the baseline budget. This increase is consistent with U.S. SOCOM's designation as the lead Combatant Command for planning, synchronizing and executing global operations against terrorist networks as specified in the 2004 Unified Command Plan. Supplemental appropriations of $5.5 billion

The AC-130 gunship's primary missions are close air support, air interdiction and force protection. The ability to call on direct fire power from the air by joint forces on the ground gives SOF a unique edge in urban and rural environments.

between Fiscal Years 2002 and 2006 contributed to improvements in dedicated SOF intelligence, surveillance and reconnaissance (ISR), organic human intelligence and technical capabilities. The Army Special Forces (SF) School increased its training throughput from 282 new active duty enlisted Special Forces personnel in 2001 to 617 new personnel in 2005 – the equivalent of an additional SF Battalion each year – with a further goal of increasing to 750 students per year. The demands of Operation Enduring Freedom and Operation Iraqi Freedom have also led to a dramatic improvement in SOF's unconventional warfare capabilities and skills.

<u>QDR Decisions</u>. To achieve the future force characteristics for SOF and build on progress to date, the Department will:

- Further increase SOF capability and capacity to conduct low-visibility, persistent presence missions and a global unconventional warfare campaign.

- Increase (starting in Fiscal Year 2007) active duty Special Forces Battalions by one-third.

- Expand Psychological Operations and Civil Affairs units by 3,700 personnel (33% increase) to provide increased support for SOF and the Army's modular forces.

- Establish a Marine Corps Special Operations Command (MARSOC) composed of 2,600 Marines and Navy personnel to train foreign military units and conduct direct action and special reconnaissance.

- Increase SEAL Team force levels to conduct direct action missions.

- Establish a SOF unmanned aerial vehicle squadron to provide organic capabilities to locate and target enemy capabilities in denied or contested areas.

- Enhance capabilities to support SOF insertion and extraction into denied areas from strategic distances.

Photo by Chief Photographer's Mate Andrew McKaskle, U.S. Navy.

A member of U.S. Navy Sea, Air, Land (SEAL) Delivery Vehicle Team prepares to launch on a training exercise from the deck of the submarine USS Philadelphia. The vehicles are one method of insertion and extraction of Special Operations Forces.

Joint Air Capabilities

Vision. Joint air capabilities must be reoriented to favor, where appropriate, systems that have far greater range and persistence; larger and more flexible payloads for surveillance or strike; and the ability to penetrate and sustain operations in denied areas. The future force will place a premium on capabilities that are responsive and survivable. It will be able to destroy moving targets in all weather conditions, exploit non-traditional intelligence and conduct next-generation electronic warfare. Joint air forces will be capable of rapidly and simultaneously locating and attacking thousands of fixed and mobile targets at global ranges. The future force will exploit stealth and advanced electronic warfare capabilities when and where they are needed. Maritime aviation will include unmanned aircraft for both surveillance and strike. Joint air capabilities will achieve a greater level of air-ground integration.

Progress to Date. Consistent with these future force characteristics, the Air Expeditionary Forces (AEF) concept has matured over the last four years, increasing personnel available for deployment by 20% (51,000). The Air Force Battlefield Airman concept has improved combat training to increase joint air-ground integration for directing air strikes in support of ground forces during conventional and irregular warfare operations. Since 2001, Air Force Joint Tactical Attack Controllers (JTACs), many attached to SOF units, have directed over 85% of air strikes in Afghanistan. The Air Force is optimizing Reserve Component personnel for new missions that can be performed from the United States, including unmanned aerial vehicle (UAV) operations and ISR reach-back, leveraging the core competencies of the reserves while reducing stress on the force.

Since 2002, the Navy and Marine Corps have integrated their tactical aircraft programs to reduce excess capacity and provide equal or greater combat capability with fewer resources. The Navy and Marine Corps have integrated their tactical aircraft squadrons within a common scheduling process to address their air requirements, achieving greater operational gains. Their integration cut potential costs by approximately $35 billion and reduced future Department of the Navy procurement by nearly 500 tactical aircraft.

The Department is continuing to reconfigure its strategic bomber fleet for enhanced conventional long-range strike missions. Satellite communications now permit the near instantaneous re-targeting of bombers and cruise missiles in flight. The integration of smart standoff weapons keeps older systems like the B-52 relevant in the modern, high-threat battlespace. New weapons provide increased capacity: the new 500-pound Joint Direct Attack Munition (JDAM) gives a single B-2 the ability to strike 80 separate targets, with precision, in all

Photo by Senior Airman Brian Ferguson, U.S. Air Force.

A B-52 Stratofortress drops live ordnance over the Nevada Test and Training Range during a firepower demonstration. In its fifth decade of service, B-52s continue to provide long-range strike capability to the joint force. The B-52 continues to be upgraded to provide new capabilities, including close air support to U.S. and partner ground forces, through the use of precision strike weapons.

weather. The Air Force has set a goal of increasing its long-range strike capabilities by 50% and the penetrating component of long-range strike by a factor of five by 2025. Approximately 45% of the future long-range strike force will be unmanned. The capacity for joint air forces to conduct global conventional strikes against time-sensitive targets will also be increased.

QDR Decisions. To achieve the future joint force characteristics and build on progress to date, the Department plans to:

- Develop a new land-based, penetrating long-range strike capability to be fielded by 2018 while modernizing the current bomber force.

- Reduce the B-52 force to 56 aircraft and use savings to fully modernize B-52s, B-1s, and B-2s to support global strike operations.

- Restructure the Joint Unmanned Combat Air System (J-UCAS) program and develop an unmanned longer-range carrier-based aircraft capable of being air-refueled to provide greater standoff capability, to expand payload and launch options, and to increase naval reach and persistence.

- Nearly double UAV coverage capacity by accelerating the acquisition of Predator UAVs and Global Hawk.

- Restructure the F-22A program and extend production through Fiscal Year 2010 with a multi-year acquisition contract, to ensure the Department does not have a gap in 5th generation stealth capabilities.

The Predator Unmanned Aerial Vehicle flies down the port side of the USS Carl Vinson. The flight was the Predator's first maritime mission with a carrier battle group and provided near-real-time infrared and color video images of the ship.

- Organize the Air Force around 86 combat wings (e.g., fighter, bomber, ISR/Battle Management/Command and Control, mobility, Air Operations Centers, Battlefield Airmen, other missions and Space/Missile) with emphasis on leveraging reach-back to minimize forward footprints and expedite force deployments, while reducing Air Force end strength by approximately 40,000 full-time equivalent personnel with balanced cuts across the Total Force.

Joint Maritime Capabilities

<u>Vision</u>. Joint maritime forces, including the Coast Guard, will conduct highly distributed operations with a networked fleet that is more capable of projecting power in the "brown and green waters" of coastal areas. They will be capable of projecting force and extending air and missile defenses from far greater ranges. Coast Guard and naval capabilities will be fully integrated. Undersea capabilities, both manned and unmanned, will use stealth, survivability, endurance, payload size and flexibility to complicate potential foes'

planning efforts and strengthen deterrence. The future force will have capabilities for conventional global strikes against time-sensitive targets. It will have greater capacity for riverine operations and other irregular operations. The future joint force will exploit the operational flexibility of seabasing to counter political anti-access and irregular warfare challenges. The Maritime Prepositioning Force (Future) family of ships will advance the capability of seabasing to support a wide spectrum of joint force operations. Special Operations Forces will exploit Afloat Forward Staging Bases (AFSB) to provide more flexible and sustainable locations from which to operate globally. The fleet will have greater presence in the Pacific Ocean, consistent with the global shift of trade and transport. Accordingly, the Navy plans to adjust its force posture and basing to provide at least six operationally available and sustainable carriers and 60% of its submarines in the Pacific to support engagement, presence and deterrence.

<u>Progress to Date</u>. Consistent with these future force characteristics, the Navy has developed and implemented several initiatives to increase the operational availability, or "employability," of

A Visit, Board, Search and Seizure team, consisting of U.S. Navy and U.S. Coast Guard sailors, approaches the starboard side of an unidentified *dhow* suspected of smuggling oil out of the Iraq Sea.

Navy and Marine Corps fleet forces. Applying distributed operating concepts, the Navy increased the number of available independent strike groups from 19 to 36. The Fleet Response Plan (FRP) modified the Navy's tiered readiness posture to increase the amount of time a ship or other naval unit is fully ready to deploy. The FRP produces adaptable force packages and sustains higher readiness throughout a unit's operational cycle, decreasing the Fleet's down time and enabling immediate deployment of six of the Navy's eleven carrier strike groups, with the addition of two more within 90 days. Rotational crewing has further increased the operational availability of forces by up to 33%.

The Navy is rapidly developing and fielding the Littoral Combat Ship (LCS) to provide an advanced littoral warfare capability. The Coast Guard is recapitalizing its deepwater ships and improving its ability to conduct joint operations with the Navy. In 2003, the Navy began converting four of the oldest nuclear ballistic missile submarines (SSBNs) to guided missile and special operations platforms. The four submarines will re-enter service by September 2007. Modifications will allow embarked Special Operations Force (SOF) personnel to penetrate denied areas to locate high-value individuals, designate targets for precision strike, or conduct direct action missions. Each submarine will also carry more than 150 Tomahawk cruise missiles.

QDR Decisions. To achieve the future joint maritime force characteristics and build on progress to date, the Department will:

The USS Florida is underway in the Atlantic Ocean. A port security Rigid Hull Inflatable Boat (RHIB) is underway off the starboard side. The USS Florida is one of four submarines being converted to a guided missile and special operations platform.

Photo by Journalist Seaman 3rd Class B.L. Keller, U.S. Navy.

- Build a larger fleet that includes 11 Carrier Strike Groups, balance the need to transform and recapitalize the fleet, improve affordability and provide stability for the shipbuilding industry.

- Accelerate procurement of Littoral Combat Ships to provide power projection capabilities in littoral waters.

- Procure the first eight ships of the Maritime Pre-Position Force (Future) to improve the Department's ability to operate in restricted access environments.

- Provide a Navy riverine capability for river patrol, interdiction and tactical troop movement on inland waterways.

- Build partner capacity to improve global maritime security by reinvigorating the Navy Foreign Area Officer program and procuring Disaster Relief Command and Control fly-away communication support capabilities.

- Return to a steady-state production rate of two attack submarines per year not later than 2012 while achieving an average per-hull procurement cost objective of $2.0 billion.

Tailored Deterrence / New Triad

<u>Vision</u>. The Department is continuing its shift from a "one size fits all" notion of deterrence toward more tailorable approaches appropriate for advanced military competitors, regional WMD states, as well as non-state terrorist networks. The future force will provide a fully balanced, tailored capability to deter both state and non-state threats – including WMD employment, terrorist attacks in the physical and information domains, and opportunistic aggression – while assuring allies and dissuading potential competitors. Consistent with the New Triad priorities developed during the 2001 Nuclear Posture Review, the force will include a wider range of non-kinetic and conventional strike capabilities, while maintaining a robust nuclear deterrent, which remains a keystone of U.S. national power. The force will also include integrated ballistic and cruise missile defenses, and a responsive infrastructure. These capabilities will be supported by a robust and responsive National Command and Control System, advanced intelligence, adaptive planning systems and an ability to maintain access to validated, high-quality information for timely situational awareness. Non-kinetic capabilities will be able to achieve some effects that currently require kinetic weapons. The Department will fight with and against computer networks as it would other weapon systems. For prompt global strike, capabilities will be available to attack fixed, hard and deeply buried, mobile and re-locatable targets with improved accuracy anywhere in the world promptly upon the President's order. Nuclear weapons will be accurate, safe and reliable, and tailored to meet modern deterrence requirements.

<u>Progress to Date</u>. Consistent with these future force characteristics, the Department has retired the Peacekeeper ICBM, removed four ballistic missile submarines from strategic nuclear service, and removed hundreds of warheads from deployed Minuteman III intercontinental ballistic missiles. The Department has fielded and deployed new conventional precision-guided munitions, including the conventionally armed Joint Air to Surface Standoff Missile and improved Tactical Tomahawk cruise missile, which can hold at risk targets that might have required nuclear forces in the past. Ballistic missile defenses have begun limited operations to defend against a range of potential threats as system development, testing, and fielding continue. In late 2004, the Navy began limited defensive operations in the Sea of Japan to identify and track ballistic missile launches aimed at the United States or its allies. U.S. efforts to expand international missile defense cooperation have also seen success. For example, the United States and Japan recently agreed in principle to cooperate in the area of missile defense through the joint development of an advanced SM-3 sea-based interceptor. The Department is working with the Department of Energy to assess the feasibility and cost of the Reliable Replacement Warhead and, if warranted, begin development of that system. This system could enable reductions in the number of older, non-deployed warheads maintained as a hedge against reliability problems in deployed systems, and assist in the evolution to a smaller and more responsive nuclear weapons infrastructure.

The U.S. Strategic Command (U.S. STRATCOM) has been assigned a number of new missions, including global strike; integration of global missile defense; space operations; integration of command, control, communications and intelligence; and combating WMD. In the information domain, the Department assigned U.S. STRATCOM responsibility for global network operations. The Assistant Secretary of Defense for Networks & Information Integration (the Department of Defense's Chief Information Officer) in coordination with U.S. STRATCOM, has developed a defense-in-depth strategy for protecting the Department's computer networks. U.S. Joint Forces Command is developing an information operations evaluation capability to integrate computer network operations into warfighting activities more effectively, consistent with its role as joint force integrator established by the Unified Command Plan of 2004.

QDR Decisions. To achieve the characteristics of the future joint force and build on progress to date, the Department will:

- Within two years, deploy an initial capability to deliver precision-guided conventional warheads using long-range Trident Submarine-Launched Ballistic Missiles.

- Reduce the number of deployed Minuteman III ballistic missiles from 500 to 450 beginning in Fiscal Year 2007.

- Retire four E-4B National Airborne Operations Center (NAOC) aircraft and accelerate procurement of two C-32 aircraft with state-of-the-art mission suites as replacement aircraft.

- Upgrade E-6B TACAMO command and control aircraft to sustain a survivable airborne link to strategic nuclear forces and provide an airborne cellular base station for domestic catastrophic events.

- Retire the U.S. STRATCOM Mobile Consolidated Command Center in Fiscal Year 2007, while funding a new distributed ground-based communications system to provide survivable and enduring command and control for nuclear forces starting in Fiscal Year 2007.

- Make additional investments in information assurance capabilities to protect information and the Department's computer networks.

A Standard Missile-3 (SM-3) is launched from the Aegis cruiser USS Lake Erie as part of a Ballistic Missile Defense System (BMDS) test to defeat a medium range ballistic missile target.

- Strengthen coordination of defensive and offensive cyber missions across the Department.

- Leverage lessons learned from computer network attack and exploitation activities to improve network defense and adopt a defense-in-depth planning approach to protect information.

- Improve the Department's information sharing with other agencies and with international allies and partners by developing information protection policies and exploiting the latest commercial technologies.

Combating WMD

<u>Vision</u>. The future force will be organized, trained, equipped, and resourced to deal with all aspects of the threat posed by weapons of mass destruction. It will have capabilities to: detect WMD, including fissile material at stand-off ranges; locate and characterize threats; interdict WMD and related shipments whether on land, at sea, or in the air; sustain operations under WMD attack; and render safe or otherwise eliminate WMD before, during or after a conflict. The Department will develop new defensive capabilities in anticipation of the continued evolution of WMD threats. Such threats include electro-magnetic pulse, man-portable nuclear devices, genetically engineered biological pathogens, and next generation chemical agents. The Department will be prepared to respond to and help other agencies to mitigate the consequences of WMD attacks.

Marines of the Decontamination Team from the Chemical Biological Incident Response Force (CBIRF) responded to anthrax attacks in Washington, D.C. CBIRF teams have also been deployed in support of Operation Iraqi Freedom and are trained to manage a host of contingences.

<u>Progress to Date</u>. Since the 2001 QDR, the Department has nearly doubled its investments in chemical and biological defenses and implemented several important organizational changes to address the challenges posed by WMD more effectively. For the next five years, beginning in Fiscal Year 2006, the Department is further increasing funding for the Chemical Biological Defense Program (CBDP) by an additional $2.1 billion (an increase of approximately 20%), focused primarily on improving its research, development and testing infrastructure as well as expanding efforts to improve defenses against emerging chemical and biological threats. In 2004, the Department led the establishment of a National BioDefense Campus at Fort Detrick, Maryland – with the U.S. Army Medical Research Institute for Infectious Diseases (USAMRIID)

and the Defense Intelligence Agency's Armed Forces Medical Intelligence Center (AFMIC) at its core – to improve cooperation among agencies conducting research and development of medical biological defenses.

In 2002, the United States led a NATO effort to establish the Alliance's multinational CBRN Defense Battalion, a unit that can provide rapidly deployable chemical, biological, radiological and nuclear (CBRN) detection, identification and hazard response support in the event of a WMD attack. This unique multinational unit became operational in July 2004. To date, more than seventeen NATO countries have contributed forces and capabilities to this battalion.

In 2003, the United States launched the Proliferation Security Initiative (PSI) as a multinational effort to interdict WMD proliferation-related shipments. Since then, more than 60 countries have begun participating in the initiative. In the past year, the United States and ten of its PSI partners have quietly cooperated on more than eleven successful WMD interdiction efforts. The Department has played a leading role in efforts to improve the operational capabilities of the United States and other PSI nations, with more than 40 countries having hosted and participated in 19 multinational PSI interdiction training exercises and gaming activities.

In 2005, the Secretary of Defense modified the Unified Command Plan by designating the Commander of U.S. Strategic Command as the lead Combatant Commander for integrating and synchronizing efforts to combat WMD.

This designation establishes for the first time a single focal point charged with integrating the Department's efforts for combating WMD in support of the geographic Combatant Commanders' operational requirements.

QDR Decisions. To achieve the characteristics of the future joint force and build on progress to date, the Department will:

- Designate the Defense Threat Reduction Agency as the primary Combat Support Agency for U.S. Strategic Command in its role as lead Combatant Commander for integrating and synchronizing combating WMD efforts.

- Expand the Army's 20th Support Command (CBRNE) capabilities to enable it to serve as a Joint Task Force capable of rapid deployment to command and control WMD elimination and site exploitation missions by 2007.

- Expand the number of U.S. forces with advanced technical render-safe skills and increase their speed of response. The Department will develop further recommendations to improve render-safe capabilities for the Fiscal Year 2008 budget.

- Improve and expand U.S. forces' capabilities to locate, track and tag shipments of WMD, missiles and related materials, including the transportation means used to move such items.

- Reallocate funding within the CBDP to invest more than $1.5 billion over the next five years to develop broad-spectrum medical counter-measures against advanced bio-terror threats, including genetically engineered intracellular bacterial pathogens and hemorrhagic fevers.

The Department will conduct this last initiative in cooperation with partner agencies utilizing the National Biodefense Campus. After leading the initial effort, the Department will pass responsibility for further research to those agencies best suited to manage medical projects.

Joint Mobility

<u>Vision</u>. Rapid global mobility is central to the effectiveness of the future force. The joint force will balance speed of deployment with desired warfighter effects to deliver the right capabilities at the right time and at the right place. Effectiveness of mobility forces will be measured not only by the quantity of material they move, but also by the operational effects they help to achieve. Mobility capabilities will be fully integrated across geographic theaters and between warfighting components and force providers, with response times measured in hours and days rather than weeks. They will enable the Department's move from a large institutional force to a future force that concentrates more operational capabilities at the front line. They will underpin the transition from a Cold War-era garrisoned force to a future force that is tailored for expeditionary operations. Future joint forces will increasingly use host-nation facilities with only a modest supporting U.S. presence, decreasing the need for traditional overseas main operating bases with large infrastructures and

reducing exposure to asymmetric threats. The U.S. overseas posture will include upgraded air support infrastructure, additional forward-deployed expeditionary maritime capabilities, long-range strike and ISR assets, and cutting-edge ground forces such as rotational Stryker units. The effective combination of seabasing, overseas presence, enhanced long-range strike, reach-back, and surge and prepositioned capabilities will reduce the forward footprint of the joint force.

U.S. Navy personnel provide perimeter security for a C-17A Globemaster III aircraft operating in support of Operation Enduring Freedom. The operation marked the first successful airlift operation by C-17 aircraft into an undeveloped dirt landing strip.

<u>Progress to Date</u>. The Department's overseas posture plan and the Integrated Global Presence and Basing Strategy informed QDR assessments of mobility priorities. In addition, the recommendations of the BRAC, now being implemented, will support overseas restructuring and the imperative of rapid power projection, with domestic basing that provides needed training infrastructure. BRAC changes will also promote joint and multi-Service basing in order to achieve economies of scale. Global mobility has made significant advances in the last decade. The Department has procured 140 of 180 contracted C-17 heavy-lift aircraft and 27 lighter

C-130Js. Both are being fielded with defensive countermeasure systems, improving their ability to operate in irregular warfare environments. The Department is also considering the acquisition of a future KC-X aircraft that will have defensive systems and provide significant cargo carrying capacity while supporting its aerial refueling mission. The U.S. Air Force is upgrading its C-5 aircraft with new engines and modernized avionics to improve fleet reliability and mission capability rates. The Department is pursuing the development of Joint High Speed Vessel (JHSV) and inter-theater high-speed sealift while maintaining sealift capabilities to support the needs of the future joint force.

QDR Decisions. In accordance with Section 131 of the Authorization Act for Fiscal Year 2006, the Department provides the following assessment of the inter-theater airlift capabilities:

- Extensive investments in cargo transportability, strategic lift, and prepositioned stocks over the past decade have yielded military forces capable of responding to a broad spectrum of security challenges worldwide.

- To maintain and enhance this capability, the Department must continue to recapitalize and modernize its mobility platforms, complete the C-17 multiyear contract, replenish prepositioned stocks consumed in recent operations, and proceed with C-5 modernization efforts. The Department plans to acquire and modernize a fleet of 292 inter-theater airlifters (180 C-17s and 112 modernized and reliability-enhanced C-5s). C-17 tooling will be moved to offsite storage to preserve the option of procuring additional C-17s.

- In addition, the Department must continue to pursue enabling technologies for transformational logistics and innovative operational concepts such as seabasing.

The Department's Mobility Capabilities Study (MCS) examined the mobility force structure needed to support the *National Defense Strategy*. Study participants included the Military Departments, the Combatant Commands, the Joint Staff and the Office of the Secretary of Defense. The study analyzed the deployment of forces to two overlapping major wars as outlined in the Joint Staff-led Operational Availability (OA) studies. It also examined concurrent demands on the mobility system associated with multiple homeland defense events and contingency operations in other theaters. Included in these latter activities are the demands associated with Special Operations Forces' worldwide operations. Additionally, both the OA studies and the MCS took into account alterations in the deployment of forces associated with the Integrated Global Presence and Basing Strategy.

The MCS and OA studies assessed the capabilities provided by a combination of forward-deployed forces, prepositioned equipment, and forces deploying from the United States. The MCS found that programmed mobility forces were capable of deploying and sustaining combat forces called for in the scenarios. The simulation exploited the air transportability of modular brigade combat teams in support of Combatant Commanders' needs. The swift employment of larger division-sized units relied upon a combination of airlift, fast sealift and prepositioned materiel. The study demonstrated the mobility system's ability to deploy these units on timelines consistent with the Combatant Commanders' needs, as well as to provide ongoing support to combat forces within the theater of operations.

To achieve the characteristics of the future joint mobility force and build on progress to date, the Department will also:

- Complete the C/KC-130 multi-year contract to procure an additional 18 Air Force C-130Js and 8 Marine Corps KC-130Js.

- Establish a joint program office for a new intra-theater light cargo aircraft for future expeditionary needs.

- Recapitalize the tanker fleet to ensure global mobility and power projection.

Intelligence, Surveillance, Reconnaissance (ISR)

Vision. The ability of the future force to establish an "unblinking eye" over the battle-space through persistent surveillance will be key to conducting effective joint operations. Future capabilities in ISR, including those operating in space, will support operations against any target, day or night, in any weather, and in denied or contested areas. The aim is to integrate global awareness with local precision. Intelligence functions will be fully integrated with operations down to the tactical level, with far greater ability to reach back

to intelligence collection systems and analytic capabilities outside the theater. Supporting this vision will require an architecture that moves intelligence data collected in the theater to the users, rather than deploying users to the theater. Future ISR capabilities will be designed to collect information that will help decision-makers mitigate surprise and anticipate potential adversaries' actions. An essential part of the future ISR architecture is a robust missile warning capability.

The future force will define ISR needs by sensor or type of intelligence needed rather than the platforms that carry the sensors or the medium in which they operate. This approach will facilitate the substitution of one capability for another to achieve the same effect, and will allow the suppliers of sensor capability to meet the needs of Combatant Commanders more efficiently. This sensor-centric approach will also improve the ability to integrate data horizontally across sensor inputs, thereby ensuring that information is available on a timely basis to a much wider range of users. Future ISR systems will employ faster and more secure technical solutions to improve the automation, integration, analysis and distribution of information to operational forces.

The United States should continue to enjoy an advantage in space capabilities across all mission areas. This advantage will be maintained by staying at least one technology generation ahead of any foreign or commercial space power. The Department will continue to develop responsive space capabilities in order to keep access to space unfettered, reliable and secure. Survivability of space capabilities will be assured by improving space situational awareness and protection, and through other space control measures. Penetrating airborne surveillance will complement space–based capabilities in order to focus on areas of interest in or near denied areas.

Progress to Date. Experience from recent operations, supported by the findings and recommendations in the 2001 QDR and a number of studies and commissions chartered by the Congress and the President – including those on national security space management, remote sensing, weapons of mass destruction and terrorism – have underscored the increasingly critical role that intelligence capabilities, including those in space, play in supporting military operations, policy and planning and acquisition decisions in the Department.

The Department has undertaken a number of organizational and operational changes, and has directed new or additional investments to increase intelligence and space capabilities and better manage the ISR resources available to the warfighter. The Department established the Under Secretary of Defense for Intelligence to provide leadership, guidance and oversight of Defense Intelligence, Security and Counterintelligence to meet Combatant Commander requirements. It also created the Executive Agent for Space and implemented steps to meet the demand for space services, including intelligence, from defense and non-defense users.

The Department has implemented measures

to strengthen human intelligence (HUMINT) capabilities, including steps to improve cultural and linguistic skills across the joint force. It is improving the integration of intelligence with operations as well as integration across intelligence disciplines (e.g., imagery, signals and human intelligence). In particular, the Department is establishing Joint Intelligence Operations Centers within the Combatant Commands and developing Intelligence Campaign Plans for all theaters. Under U.S. STRATCOM, the Department established a functional command to synchronize strategy and planning and integrate all national, theater and tactical ISR capabilities.

Photo by Specialist Johnny R. Aragon, U.S. Army

A U.S. military intelligence officer (middle) and Afghan military intelligence soldier (right) speak privately with the elder of a village (left) in the Shah Wali Ko District, Afghanistan. Coalition Forces are building capacity of indigenous forces, forging relationships with local leaders and preventing Taliban attempts to reestablish themselves in the area.

To manage more effectively the Department's intelligence resources, the Department has approved the creation of a Military Intelligence Program and is implementing an enhanced Defense Civilian Intelligence Personnel System to better compete for, develop and retain the professional intelligence workforce. The Department has increased the number of intelligence professionals working in collection and analytical disciplines to support growth in homeland defense and war on terror missions.

Combat Support Agencies have also relocated or deployed significant numbers of intelligence analysts, intelligence collectors and collection managers to areas where they can be of greatest value to their customers.

QDR Decisions. To achieve the future joint force characteristics and build on progress to date, the Department will:

- Improve both the capability and capacity of defense human intelligence assets to identify terrorists and characterize and penetrate their networks, in cooperation with other government agencies and international partners.

- Increase measurement and signature intelligence (MASINT) capabilities to identify enemy WMD and their delivery systems, and to support other applications.

- Expand signals intelligence (SIGINT) collection with sufficient revisit rate and geo-location capabilities for military operations. The Aerial Common Sensor (ACS) program will be restructured as the Department explores a new tri-service solution to meet "multi-intelligence" requirements.

- Fund the U.S. contribution to establish a NATO Intelligence Fusion Center.

- Increase investment in unmanned aerial vehicles to provide more flexible capabilities to identify and track moving targets in denied areas.

- Realign capabilities to free up resources for next generation systems and modernize and sustain selected legacy systems (e.g., a new engine for the Joint Surveillance Target Attack Radar System).

- Implement a new imagery intelligence approach focused on achieving persistent collection capabilities in cooperation with the Director of National Intelligence. Investments in moving target indicator and synthetic aperture radar capabilities, including Space Radar, will grow to provide a highly persistent capability to identify and track moving ground targets in denied areas.

The Space Radar program (in development) will provide persistent, all-weather, day and night surveillance and reconnaissance capabilities in denied areas for the Department of Defense and the Intelligence Community. (Artist's conception)

- Balance air- and space-borne ISR capabilities and integrate them with other forces, and investigate the use of high-altitude loitering capabilities.

- Fully fund E-10A technology demonstrator while terminating procurement.

- Improve responsive space access, satellite operations, and other space enabling capabilities such as the space industrial base, space science and technology efforts, and the space professional cadre.

- Increase Maritime Domain Awareness through improved integration with interagency and international partners, and accelerated investment in multinational information sharing systems such as the Automatic Identification System and the Multinational Information Sharing System.

Achieving Net-Centricity

Vision. Harnessing the power of information connectivity defines net-centricity. By enabling critical relationships between organizations and people, the Department is able to accelerate the speed of business processes, operational decision-making and subsequent actions. Recent operational experiences in Afghanistan and Iraq have demonstrated the value of net-centric operations. Ground forces were able to reach back to remote UAV pilots in Nevada to direct UAVs in support of their operations, achieving a level of air-ground integration that was difficult to imagine just a decade ago. Such connectivity is helping joint forces gain greater situational awareness to attack the enemy.

Achieving the full potential of net-centricity requires viewing information as an enterprise asset to be shared and as a weapon system to be protected. As an enterprise asset, the collection and dissemination of information should be managed by portfolios of capabilities that cut across legacy stove-piped systems. These capability portfolios would include network-based command and control, communications on the move and information fusion. Current and evolving threats highlight the need to design, operate and defend the network to ensure continuity of joint operations.

Progress to Date. The foundation for net-centric operations is the Global Information Grid (GIG), a globally interconnected, end-to-end set of trusted and protected information networks. The GIG optimizes the processes for collecting, processing, storing, disseminating, managing and sharing information within the Department and with other partners. The Department has made steady progress implementing net-centric systems and concepts of operation. It has deployed an enhanced land-based network and new satellite constellation as part of the Transformational Communication Architecture to provide high-bandwidth, survivable internet protocol communications. Together, they will support battle-space awareness, time-sensitive targeting and communications on the move. Deployed

Photo by Photographer's Mate Airman Dominique V. Brown, U.S. Navy.

Air Traffic Controllers stand watch in the Carrier Air Traffic Control Center aboard the USS Nimitz. The collection and sharing of information such as that obtained by the USS Nimitz in support of Maritime Security Operations denies terrorists use of the maritime environment as a venue for attack or to transport personnel, weapons or other material.

terminals – from command and control (Joint Tactical Radio System) to very large bandwidth ISR systems – are extending the communications "backbone" down to the smallest tactical unit in the field. The Department has also implemented a data strategy enabling the fusion of information from any platform or terminal. Pulling all this together, the revised Unified Command Plan has assigned U.S. STRATCOM lead responsibility to operate and protect the Department's Global Information Grid.

QDR Decisions. To move closer toward this vision and build on progress to date, the Department will:

- Strengthen its data strategy – including the development of common data lexicons, standards, organization, and categorization – to improve information sharing and information assurance, and extend it across a multitude of domains, ranging from intelligence to personnel systems.

- Increase investment to implement the GIG, defend and protect information and networks and focus research and development on its protection.

- Develop an information-sharing strategy to guide operations with Federal, state, local and coalition partners.

- Shift from Military Service-focused efforts toward a more Department-wide enterprise net-centric approach, including expansion of the Distributed Common Ground System.

- Restructure the Transformational Satellite (TSAT) program to "spiral develop" its capabilities and re-phase launches accordingly, and add resources to increase space-based relay capacity.

- Develop an integrated approach to ensure alignment in the phasing and pacing of terminals and space vehicles.

- Develop a new bandwidth requirements model to determine optimal network size and capability to best support operational forces.

The master air attack plan (MAAP) toolkit is an example of software tools that will improve accuracy and facilitate planning. The toolkit is designed to make production of the MAAP and subsequent air tasking order quicker and less prone to error.

Joint Command and Control

Vision. The joint force of the future will have more robust and coherent joint command and control capabilities. Rapidly deployable, standing joint task force headquarters will be available to the Combatant Commanders in greater numbers to meet the range of potential contingencies. These headquarters will enable the real-time synthesis of operations and intelligence functions and processes, increasing joint force adaptability and speed of action. The joint headquarters will have better information, processes and tools to design and conduct network-enabled operations with other agencies and with international partners. Implementation of Adaptive Planning in the Department will further enhance the lethality of both subordinate standing joint task force headquarters and their parent Combatant Commands by enabling them to produce high-quality, relevant plans in as little as six months. Adaptive Planning is the catalyst that will transform the Department's operational planning processes and systems. Furthermore, Global Force Management, the Department's model for force management, reporting and analysis, will provide Commanders with an unprecedented depth of up-to-date and decision-quality information on unit readiness, personnel and equipment availability.

Progress to Date. Since 2001, the Department has made marked progress towards strengthening joint operations as a focus of defense transformation. The activation of standing joint task force headquarters has improved the ability of the force to respond to crises. With a "core element" – a standing command and control team with functional and geographic expertise – these headquarters provide peacetime planning capabilities for contingencies, a departure from past practices of implementing ad hoc approaches after crises occur. The first Standing Joint Force Headquarters (core element) was established in 2004 and has since deployed to Iraq, the Horn of Africa and to relief efforts associated with Hurricane Katrina and the Pakistani earthquake. The implementation of Global

Force Management, by integrating data on worldwide availability and readiness, allows the Department's leadership to source forces flexibly for operations, regardless of where they are located or what command they have traditionally supported.

QDR Decisions. To achieve the characteristics of the future joint force and build on progress to date, the Department will:

- Transform designated existing Service operational headquarters to fully functional and scalable Joint Command and Control Joint Task Force-capable Headquarters beginning in Fiscal Year 2007.

- Establish a second operationally ready and immediately deployable Standing Joint Force Headquarters core element at the U.S. Joint Forces Command consistent with its responsibilities as Joint Force Integrator under the 2004 Unified Command Plan.

- Automate and link key planning processes in a networked, virtual environment to enable real-time collaboration and rapid production of high-quality planning products.

- Implement Adaptive Planning across the Department by increasing the number of fully qualified planners, investing in advanced planning toolsets, and organizing planning staffs to exploit the advantages that new technology and highly trained, experienced planners provide.

- Increase resources to develop software, tactics,

techniques, procedures and other initiatives needed to support the Global Force Management System.

RESHAPING THE DEFENSE ENTERPRISE

Just as we must transform America's military capability to meet changing threats, we must transform the way the Department works and what it works on. We must build a Department where each of the dedicated people here can apply their immense talents to defend America, where they have the resources, information and freedom to perform... It demands agility—more than today's bureaucracy allows. And that means we must recognize another transformation: the revolution in management, technology and business practices. Successful modern businesses are leaner and less hierarchical than ever before. They reward innovation and they share information. They have to be nimble in the face of rapid change or they die.

> *Donald H. Rumsfeld, Secretary of Defense,*
> *September 10, 2001*

To win the long war, the Department of Defense must reshape the defense enterprise in ways that better support the warfighter and are appropriate for the threat environment. Today, the armed forces are hampered by inefficient business practices. The Department's current structure and processes are handicaps in the protracted fight we now face against agile and networked foes. Over the last twenty years, the Department has increasingly integrated its warfighting concepts, organization, training and operations to create the world's most formidable joint force. Sustaining continuous operational change and innovation are a hallmark of U.S. forces. The Department's organizations, processes and enabling authorities urgently require a similar

transformation. The Department's approach is to improve significantly organizational effectiveness, and in so doing, reap the rewards of improved efficiencies.

The 2001 QDR highlighted the loss of resources, in terms of people and dollars, caused by inefficiencies in the Department's support functions. The Department responded with a comprehensive effort to streamline business and decision-making processes, with the express goal of better supporting the joint warfighter. Since 2001, the Department has moved steadily toward a more integrated and transparent senior decision-making culture and process for both operational and investment matters. The Department has made substantial strides in fostering joint solutions, including the creation of new organizations and processes that cut across traditional stovepipes. It has standardized business rules and data structures for common use. Most importantly, the Department has made notable progress toward an outcome-oriented, capabilities-based planning approach that provides the joint warfighter with the capabilities needed to address a wider range of asymmetric challenges.

Recent operational experiences have demonstrated the need to bring further agility, flexibility and horizontal integration to the defense support infrastructure. The Department has responded to that need with several innovations in its organizations and support services. Three examples of such innovations are the Joint Improvised Explosive Device (IED) Defeat Task Force, the Joint Rapid Acquisition

Cell and improved supply-chain logistics.

In both Iraq and Afghanistan, the terrorist weapon of choice remains the improvised explosive device, normally taking the form of roadside bombs, suicide car bombs and a variety of remotely initiated devices. To counter the threat posed by these weapons, the Department created the Joint IED Defeat Task Force. The Task Force unified all Department efforts to defeat IEDs, combining the best technology solutions with relevant intelligence and innovative operating methods. In Fiscal Year 2005, the Department invested more than $1.3 billion in IED Defeat initiatives, including counter-radio controlled IED electronic warfare, IED surveillance, the Joint IED Defeat Center of Excellence, counter-bomber programs and stand-off IED detection and neutralization. The Task Force has also provided funds for training to military units en route to operational theaters as well as expert field teams that work directly with units in Iraq and Afghanistan. Since the Task Force's inception, the Department has decreased the IED casualty rate by a factor of two.

A Talon 3B tracked robot waits for its next command after an improvised explosive device was detonated in Baghdad, Iraq. The increasing use of robotics has improved U.S. force protection significantly in Operation Iraqi Freedom.

The Joint Rapid Acquisition Cell (JRAC) is another innovation that grew out of U.S. experiences in Iraq and Afghanistan. The Department's standard processes for providing materiel and logistics proved too slow and cumbersome to meet the immediate needs of forces in the field. Recognizing this deficiency, the Secretary of Defense established a cell dedicated to finding actionable solutions to urgent warfighter needs. The JRAC has supported efforts that provided military personnel key force protection items such as the Advanced Combat Helmet, lightweight Global Positioning System receivers, improved ammunition packs and individual weapon optics. Working with the Military Departments and Combatant Commands, this initiative has accelerated development and delivery of more than a dozen critical programs, from intelligence collection and dissemination to enhanced force protection.

Improved support to the warfighter has occurred in the logistics chain as well. The Department vested leadership of the complex distribution process in a single owner, the U.S. Transportation Command (U.S. TRANSCOM). Exercising its new role, U.S. TRANSCOM established a Deployed Distribution Operations Center in Kuwait to speed the flow of materiel into Iraq and Afghanistan in support of coalition operations. The Center quickly assembled a team of logistics experts and gave them authority to direct air and seaport operations and cross-country moves in the theater. Lead times for stocked items dropped by more than 45% since the peaks recorded in 2003. Better synchronization of transportation assets allowed the Army to cut costs by $268 million in

Fiscal Year 2004. On-time delivery rates are now at over 90%. The Center's process innovations improved mission performance at less cost to the Department and the American taxpayer.

Department reforms since 2001, including those innovations born of wartime necessity, represent the types of changes the QDR has sought to accelerate.

Toward A New Defense Enterprise

The Department's enterprise reforms are guided by a three-part vision:

- First, the Department must be responsive to its stakeholders. Not only must the Department's support functions enhance the U.S. military's ability to serve the President and provide a strong voice for the joint warfighter, it must also provide the best possible value to the American taxpayer. The Department will work to improve effectiveness dramatically across civilian and military functions as the foundation for increased efficiency.

- Second, the Department must provide information and analysis necessary to make timely and well-reasoned decisions. The Department's culture, authorities, and organizations must be aligned in a manner that facilitates, rather than hinders, effective decision-making and enables responsive mission execution while maintaining accountability. Improved horizontal integration will be critical to the Department's success.

- Third, the Department must undertake

reforms to reduce redundancies and ensure the efficient flow of business processes. As we capitalize on existing transformational efforts across the enterprise, we will continually evaluate support systems and processes to optimize their responsiveness.

To achieve this vision and produce strategy-driven outcomes, the Department's roles and responsibilities, and those of each of its component organizations, must be clearly delineated. Roles and responsibilities within the Department of Defense fall into roughly three categories. At the senior-most levels, leaders are concerned with *governance* – setting strategy, prioritizing enterprise efforts, assigning responsibilities and authorities, allocating resources and communicating a shared vision. In order to meet the strategic objectives set out by the Department's senior leadership, some components act in a *management* role, focusing on organizing tasks, people, relationships and technology. The vast majority of the Department's personnel then *work* to execute the strategy and plans established at management level.

In the 2006 QDR, the Department looked across these three levels of responsibility – governance, management and work – to ensure that organizations, processes and authorities are well aligned.

Governance Reforms

Senior Leadership Focus

A key measure of success is the extent to which the Department's senior leadership is able to fulfill the following functions:

- <u>Strategic Direction</u> – Identify the key outputs – not inputs – they expect from the Department's components and determine the appropriate near-, mid-, and long-term strategies for achieving them. Such outputs will be focused on the needs of the President as Commander in Chief and the joint warfighters.

- <u>Identity</u> – Establish an organizational culture that fosters innovation and excellence. Communicate the Department's strategy, policy and institutional ethos to the internal workforce and to external audiences.

- <u>Capital Acquisition and Macro Resource Allocation</u> – Shape the Department's major investments in people, equipment, concepts and organizations to support the Nation's objectives most effectively.

- <u>Corporate Decision Making</u> – Implement agile and well-aligned governance, management and work processes. Ensure the Department has the processes, tools and transparent analyses to support decisions.

- <u>Performance Assessment</u> – Monitor performance to ensure strategic alignment and make adjustments to strategic direction based on performance.

- <u>Force Employment</u> – Determine how U.S. forces are utilized and meet the day-to-day oversight needs of the joint force. Operational matters are the responsibility of the joint warfighters. The Department's senior civilian and military leaders ensure that forces are employed in ways that meet the President's strategic objectives.

The Department will work to better align processes, structures and, as necessary, authorities to improve its senior leaders' ability to govern in these core areas. Today, the Office of the Secretary of Defense and the Joint Staff perform many functions beyond those identified above, including program management and execution. To ensure that senior leadership can maintain focus on the key governance issues elaborated above, the Department will identify management and execution activities currently being conducted at the governance level and consider them for elimination or realignment.

<u>Build Capability to Inform Strategic Choice</u>

To better support the joint warfighter, the Department is launching several initiatives to integrate the processes that define needed capabilities, identify solutions and allocate resources to acquire them. The following four interrelated reforms emphasize the need for improved information-sharing and collaboration.

First, the Department will implement a more transparent, open and agile decision-making process. To do this, common authoritative information sources will be identified, Department-level financial databases will be combined, and common analytic methods will be adopted. For example, the Department is testing a number of tools that could provide common capability views using existing resource and programming databases. One such pilot project is a transparent integrated air and missile defense database. Experimenting through such pilots, the Department will seek to identify and rapidly develop preferred capability area solutions that will facilitate open and agile decision-making.

Second, the Department will reach investment decisions through collaboration among the joint warfighter, acquisition and resource communities. Joint warfighters will assess needs in terms of desired effects and the time frame in which capabilities are required. Assessments of potential solutions should be informed by the acquisition community's judgment of technological feasibility and cost-per-increment of capability improvement, and by the resource community's assessment of affordability. These inputs will be provided early in the decision-making process, before significant resources are committed. Once an investment decision has been approved, changes will require collaboration among all three communities at the appropriate decision level to ensure strategy-driven, affordable and achievable outcomes.

A recent, much-needed restructuring of the troubled Joint Tactical Radio System (JTRS) program exemplifies this collaborative approach. Because the radio system must be interoperable with other systems across the full spectrum of the joint force, decisions regarding the future of the JTRS program had profound effects throughout the Department. To ensure a solution that will meet the joint warfighter's needs and provide best value to the taxpayer, the warfighting and acquisition communities worked closely together to develop the investment strategy and

the Military Departments contributed needed resources for the restructuring.

Third, the Department will begin to break out its budget according to joint capability areas. Using such a joint capability view – in place of a Military Department or traditional budget category display – should improve the Department's understanding of the balancing of strategic risks and required capability trade-offs associated with particular decisions. The Department has already developed and tested at U.S. Pacific Command an automated process that maps resource needs to discrete operational plans and missions. For the first time, a Combatant Commander is able to ascertain the resource requirements associated with particular capabilities, such as striking fleeting targets. The Department is working to expand on this program to enable Department-wide assessment of capability areas and facilitate capability portfolio management and will explore this approach with the Congress.

Fourth, to manage the budget allocation process with accountability, an acquisition reform study initiated by the Deputy Secretary of Defense recommended the Department work with the Congress to establish "Capital Accounts" for Major Acquisition Programs. The purpose of capital budgeting is to provide stability in the budgeting system and to establish accountability for acquisition programs throughout the hierarchy of program responsibility from the program manager, through the Service Acquisition Executive, the Secretaries of the Military Departments and the Office of the Secretary of Defense.

Together, these improvements should enable senior leaders to implement a risk-informed investment strategy reflecting joint warfighting priorities.

Aligning Authority and Accountability through Joint Capability Portfolios

Most of the Department's resources are provided through the Military Services. This arrangement can lead both to gaps or redundancies within capability areas as each Service attempts to supply a complete warfighting package rather than organize to depend on capabilities provided by other Military Departments. To optimize the provision of capabilities for the joint warfighter, the Department will work to re-orient its processes around joint capability portfolios. In the acquisition realm, the Department has already instituted several joint capability reviews. These reviews look across major force programs to assess needed investments in specific capability portfolio areas such as integrated air and missile defense, land attack weapons and electronic warfare.

The QDR used such a portfolio approach to evaluate surveillance capabilities. The Department began by accounting for all of its current and planned surveillance capabilities and programs. This included a transparent review of capabilities at all levels of classification. Viewing capabilities across the entire portfolio of assets enabled decision-makers to make informed choices about how to reallocate resources among previously stove-piped programs, to deliver needed capabilities to the joint force more rapidly and efficiently.

The Department will build on these initial efforts to integrate tasks, people, relationships, technologies and associated resources more effectively across the Department's many activities. By shifting the focus from Service-specific programs to joint capabilities, the Department should be better positioned to understand the implications of investment and resource trade-offs among competing priorities. As a first step, the Department will manage three capability areas using a capability portfolio concept: Joint Command and Control, Joint Net-Centric Operations and Joint Space Operations. As we learn from experience and gain confidence in this approach, we plan to expand it to other capability areas.

High Speed Vessel Two participated in a 2003 exercise with West African nations. The follow-on Joint High Speed Vehicle (J-HSV) is a joint experiment between the Navy, Marines, Army and Special Operations Command utilizing a modified high speed, lightweight commercial ferry produced in Australia for potential U.S. military usage. Future variants of the J-HSV will provide a capability to transport significant ground forces at high speeds into shallow water ports without modern unloading equipment.

Managing Joint Task Assignments

Effective governance is facilitated by the clear alignment of authority, responsibility and resources at the management level. Some of the most difficult challenges in governance arise when joint management arrangements cut across the traditional and often statutory authority structure of the Military Departments and Defense Agencies. The establishment of the Combatant Commands created new sources of demand for joint capabilities separate from the organizations with responsibility to supply them.

For example, when a program or mission is identified as a priority area, the Secretary may choose to direct an organization to manage or resource the joint effort for the Department. In the past, this has been accomplished by designating a component or activity as the "Executive Agent" – a term the meaning of which varies widely from one arrangement to the next. When the responsibilities for joint management activities are not clearly defined or strategically aligned, implementation is problematic and resources are used less efficiently.

This QDR underscores the need for a better way to organize and manage joint activities to ensure that mission assignment is accompanied by the authorities, resources and clear performance expectations necessary for mission success. Consequently, the Department is implementing a disciplined process for assigning joint missions and tasks and evaluating their resource priority. The Joint Task Assignment Process will centrally assign and oversee joint management arrangements to ensure joint activities are aligned to the Department's strategic objectives; designated with the proper authorities, responsibilities and resources; effectively structured to minimize overlaps and gaps; established with clear lines of accountability; and

continually assessed for performance and need.

Driving Business Transformation

The Defense Business Systems Management Committee (DBSMC) was established to improve governance of the Department's business transformation effort. The DBSMC is a top-level, single point-of-decision mechanism that brings together senior leaders from across the enterprise to drive business process change and improve support to the joint warfighter. The Department also developed an Enterprise Transition Plan and associated Architecture to guide transformation of the Department's business operations. The DBSMC will govern execution of the Enterprise Transition Plan by ensuring accountability and increasing senior leadership direction.

To ensure alignment with the business transformation strategy, the Department has created Investment Review Boards to evaluate programs of record against the Enterprise Architecture. Funds cannot be obligated for any business system investment not certified by the appropriate official and approved by the DBSMC to be in compliance with the Department's architecture.

More recently, the Defense Business Transformation Agency (BTA) was created to integrate and oversee corporate-level business systems and initiatives. The BTA is the management link responsible for integrating work across the Department in areas such as human resources, financial management, acquisition, and logistics. It is accountable to the DBSMC governing body for results.

Managing Risks and Measuring Performance Across the Enterprise

In the 2001 QDR, the Department introduced a risk management framework to enable the Department's senior leadership to better balance near-term demands against preparations for the future. This balanced risk approach has been successfully implemented in a number of organizations throughout the Department to guide strategic planning and day-to-day management. The Department is now taking advantage of lessons learned from this initial implementation phase to refine and develop a more robust framework to enable decision-making.

The Department will reevaluate its enterprise-wide outcome goals to maintain strategic alignment and ensure the Department's objectives are clearly set forth. The Department will also evaluate and develop or refine the metrics to measure efforts to implement the strategy to provide useful information to senior leadership. Improved metrics will allow senior leaders at the governance level to manage by exception— monitoring the overall health of the organization and focusing attention on areas needing top-level direction and support. Each level of the enterprise is accountable for measuring performance and delivering results that support the Department-wide strategy. Organizations must have the autonomy needed to perform within guidance, but with adequate oversight to ensure strategic alignment.

Additional Governance Reforms

The Department is considering additional initiatives aimed at improving governance in each of the five corporate focus areas. These include the following:

- Designating a single lead advocate for the future joint warfighter in order to improve the Department's long-range, joint perspective on the requirements, acquisition and resource allocation processes.

- Creating new horizontal organizations to better integrate the Department's activities in key areas, including strategic communication and human capital strategy.

- Migrating toward a shared services model for support functions, such as administration, management and computer support.

Although reforms cannot occur overnight, the course is clear. The complex strategic environment demands that our structure and processes be streamlined and integrated to better support the President and joint warfighter. The Department is committed to doing so.

Management and Work Reforms

Beyond governance, this QDR identified opportunities for continued transformation of acquisition and logistics processes.

Improving Defense Acquisition Performance

There is a growing and deep concern in the Department of Defense's senior leadership and in the Congress about the acquisition processes. This lack of confidence results from an inability to determine accurately the true state of major acquisition programs when measured by cost, schedule and performance. The unpredictable nature of Defense programs can be traced to instabilities in the broader acquisition system. Fundamentally reshaping that system should make the state of the Department's major acquisition programs more predictable and result in better stewardship of the U.S. tax dollar. There are several ongoing reviews of defense acquisition improvements being conducted both within and outside the Department in an effort to address these issues. Their results will inform the Department's efforts to reshape defense acquisition into a truly 21st century process that is responsive to the joint warfighter.

The Department of Defense is focusing on bringing the needed capabilities to the joint force more rapidly, by fashioning a much more effective acquisition system and associated set of processes. The Department is considering adopting a risk-based source selection process in place of the current cost-based approach. Source selection decisions would not use cost as the sole criteria but rather would be based on technical and management risk. Effectively balancing cost, technical risk and management realities would require closer integration of the Department's joint capabilities identification, resource allocation and acquisition processes, with clear responsibilities defined for each.

In an effort to ensure needed capabilities are fielded rapidly, acquisition development and procurement programs will shift to a time-certain approach. Early in program development, senior leaders will make the key trade-offs necessary to balance performance, time and available resources. Upgrades and improvements can be added in subsequent spirals based on the maturity of the technology. Combining time-certain development and procurement of capability with a risk-based approach to source selection should provide much greater stability in the acquisition system. Stability should allow for more predictable acquisition programs measured by cost, schedule and performance.

Managing Supply Chain Logistics

In response to the 2001 QDR, the Department undertook a number of initiatives to improve the effectiveness and efficiency with which the Department moves and sustains military forces. These initiatives included efforts to improve the deployment process and reduce the logistics footprint and its associated costs. The

A C-130 drops supplies during an operation intended to prevent reemergence of terrorist activities in Afghanistan. U.S. and partner forces remain vigilant in combating any new terrorist extremist forces.

Department also worked to provide standing joint force headquarters with an integrated logistics picture and accelerated the creation and use of logistics decision-support tools. In the past four years, the Department has markedly increased the integration of field exercises and experimentation with the processes for determining logistics systems, doctrine and force structure requirements. In addition, as noted earlier, the Department is changing its logistics processes and procedures as dictated by the needs of current operations.

As a result of these initiatives, the Department has made significant strides in migrating to a capabilities-based logistics approach. In this QDR, the Department focused on improving visibility into supply chain logistics costs and performance and on building a foundation for continuous improvements in performance. The strategy for achieving these objectives starts by linking resources to supply chain logistics activities in order to understand the costs they entail. The Department must also assess commercial supply chain metrics as potential performance targets to bring down the costs and to speed the delivery of needed items. Promising ongoing initiatives, such as the single deployment process owner, must be continually improved and accelerated. Lastly, there is a need to develop realistic and defendable strategic performance targets for focused logistics capabilities to guide both capital investment and process improvement.

The Department is implementing a number of specific initiatives aimed at meeting supply chain objectives. For example, the use of active and passive Radio Frequency Identification (RFID) technologies will play a key role in achieving the Department's vision for implementing knowledge-enabled logistics support to the warfighter through automated asset visibility and management. RFID is designed to enable the sharing, integration and synchronizing of data from the strategic to the tactical level, informing every node in the supply chain network. This information should provide greater insight into the cause-and-effect relationship between resources and readiness. Such fact-based insights, coupled with the implementation of continuous process improvement tools like Lean, Six Sigma and Performance Based Logistics, will help optimize the productive output of the overall Department of Defense supply chain.

Transforming the Medical Health System (MHS)

New breakthroughs in science and health, and new innovations in prevention and wellness, offer the opportunity to develop a 21st century Military Health System that will improve health and save both lives and money. This transformation in health and healthcare parallels other transformations in the Department of Defense. It is the Department's goal to have a lifetime relationship with the entire Department of Defense family which maximizes prevention, wellness and personal choices and responsibility. As with other areas related to the Department enterprise, the QDR recommends aligning medical support with emerging joint force employment concepts. Building on recent improvements in new purchased care contracts and the streamlining of regional TRICARE management structures, the QDR recommends continuing to shift toward a market-driven, performance-based investment program. It also recommends improving planning processes and the transparency of information, while leveraging the recent launch of the Department's electronic health record system. This new system is needed to effectively manage MHS by adopting a more flexible financing process. Above all, the Department's military and civilian senior leaders endorse the need to modernize the TRICARE benefit structure for those customers who are not on Active Duty. The intent is to promote longer and healthier retirement lives by encouraging self-responsibility for their own and their family's health and the use of health resources to achieve the longest, healthiest lives at the lowest cost. Doing so will require changes in legislation and rules to adjust TRICARE cost-sharing features so that they restore the balance Congress created in establishing the TRICARE program in the 1990's and also to seek authority for Health Savings Accounts.

Summary

Without a doubt, reshaping the defense enterprise is difficult. The structures and processes developed over the past half-century were forged in the Cold War and strengthened by success in it. However, the strategic landscape of the 21ˢᵗ century demands excellence across a much broader set of national security challenges. With change comes turmoil, and achieving a desired vision requires determination and perseverance within the Department and, importantly, cooperation with the Congress. As

we emphasize agility, flexibility, responsiveness and effectiveness in the operational forces, so too must the Department's organizations, processes and practices embody these characteristics if they are to support the joint warfighter and our Commander in Chief.

DEVELOPING A 21ˢᵗ CENTURY TOTAL FORCE

The Department of Defense is the world's largest employer, directly employing more than three million people. The Department's Total Force – its active and reserve military components, its civil servants, and its contractors – constitutes its warfighting capability and capacity. Members of the Total Force serve in thousands of locations around the world, performing a vast array of duties to accomplish critical missions.

No prudent military commander wants a fair fight, seeking instead to "overmatch" adversaries in cunning, capability and commitment. The selfless service and heroism of the men and women of the well-trained all-volunteer Total Force has been a primary source of U.S. strategic overmatch in confronting the wide range of threats we face and a key to successful military operations over the past several decades. The Total Force must continue to adapt to different operating environments, develop new skills and rebalance its capabilities and people if it is to

remain prepared for the new challenges of an uncertain future.

Recent operational experiences highlight capabilities and capacities that the Department must instill in the Total Force to prevail in a long, irregular war while deterring a broad array of challenges. The future force must be more finely tailored, more accessible to the joint commander and better configured to operate with other agencies and international partners in complex operations. It must have far greater endurance. It must be trained, ready to operate and able to make decisions in traditionally non-military areas, such as disaster response and stabilization. Increasing the adaptability of the Total Force while also reducing stress on military personnel and their families is a top priority for the Department. These imperatives require a new strategy for shaping the Department's Total Force, one that will adjust policies and authorities while introducing education and training initiatives to equip civilian and military warfighters to overmatch any future opponent.

The Department and Military Services must carefully distribute skills among the four elements of the Total Force (Active Component, Reserve Component, civilians and contractors) to optimize their contributions across the range of military operations, from peace to war. In a reconfigured Total Force, a new balance of skills must be coupled with greater accessibility to people so that the right forces are available at the right time. Both uniformed and civilian personnel must be readily available to joint commanders.

Photo by Photographer's Mate 3rd Class Rebecca J. Moat, U.S. Navy.

An officer assigned to Navy hospital ship USNS Mercy explains her rank insignia to Indonesian military and civilian nurses after instructing them in cardiopulmonary resuscitation (CPR). USNS Mercy operated off the coast of Sumatra, Indonesia, providing assistance to international relief organizations; it hosted medical teams operating ashore in areas affected by the Indian Ocean tsunami.

Photo by Captain Dave Huxsoll, U.S. Air Force.

A Department of Defense contractor (left) and U.S. Air Force personnel (right) provide first aid to an Afghan girl at the Bagrami Village refugee camp in Kabul, Afghanistan. Providing essential aid is a critical part of the reconstruction effort and employs all elements of the Total Force.

This operational Total Force must remain prepared for complex operations at home or abroad, including working with other U.S. agencies, allies, partners and non-governmental organizations. Routine integration with foreign and domestic counterparts requires new forms of advanced joint training and education.

Finally, the Department must effectively compete with the civilian sector for high-quality personnel. The transformation of the Total Force will require updated, appropriate authorities and tools from Congress to shape it and improve its sustainability. Two key enablers of this transformation will be a new *Human Capital Strategy* for the Department, and the application of the new National Security Personnel System to manage the Department's civilian personnel.

Reconfiguring the Total Force

Recent operational experiences in Iraq and Afghanistan highlight the need to rebalance military skills between and within the Active and Reserve Components. Accordingly, over the past several years, the Military Departments are rebalancing – shifting, transferring or eliminating – approximately 70,000 positions within or between the Active and Reserve Components. The Department plans to rebalance an additional 55,000 military personnel by 2010. The Military Departments are applying this same scrutiny across the Total Force to ensure that the right skills reside inside each element. The Military Departments and Combatant Commanders will continually assess the force to ensure it remains responsive to meet future demands. U.S. Joint Forces Command (U.S. JFCOM), as the joint force provider, is aiding the effort by ensuring the appropriate global distribution of ready forces and competencies. The Department plans to introduce a new methodology and review process to establish a baseline for personnel policy, including the development of joint metrics and a common lexicon to link the Defense Strategy to Service-level rebalancing decisions. This process will help synchronize rebalancing efforts across the Department.

A Continuum of Service

The traditional, visible distinction between war and peace is less clear at the start of the 21ˢᵗ century. In a long war, the United States expects to face large and small contingencies at unpredictable intervals. To fight the long war and conduct other future contingency operations, joint force commanders need to have more immediate access to the Total Force. In particular, the Reserve Component must be operationalized, so that select Reservists and units are more accessible and more readily deployable than today. During the Cold War, the Reserve Component was used, appropriately, as a "strategic reserve," to provide support to Active Component forces during major combat operations. In today's global context, this concept is less relevant. As a result, the Department will:

- Pursue authorities for increased access to the Reserve Component: to increase the period authorized for Presidential Reserve Call-up from 270 to 365 days.

- Better focus the use of the Reserve Components' competencies for homeland defense and civil support operations, and seek changes to authorities to improve access to Guard and reserve consequence management capabilities and capacity in support of civil authorities.

- Achieve revision of Presidential Reserve Call-Up authorities to allow activation of Military Department Reserve Components for natural disasters in order to smooth the process for meeting specific needs without relying solely on volunteers.

- Allow individuals who volunteer for activation on short notice to serve for long periods on major headquarters staffs as individual augmentees.

- Develop select reserve units that train more intensively and require shorter notice for deployment.

Additionally, the Military Departments will explore the creation of all-volunteer reserve units with high-demand capabilities, and the Military

Departments and Combatant Commanders will expand the concept of contracted volunteers.

Building the Right Skills

Maintaining the capabilities required to conduct effective multi-dimensional joint operations is fundamental to the U.S. military's ability to overmatch adversaries. Both battlefield integration with interagency partners and combined operations – the integration of the joint force and coalition forces – will be standard features in future operations. The combination of joint, combined and interagency capabilities in modern warfare represents the next step in the evolution of joint warfighting and places new demands on the Department's training and education processes.

Joint Training

The QDR assessed and compared the joint training capabilities of each of the Military Departments. Although the Military Departments have established operationally proven processes and standards, it is clear that further advances in joint training and education are urgently needed to prepare for complex, multinational and interagency operations in the future. Toward this end, the Department will:

- Develop a Joint Training Strategy to address new mission areas, gaps and continuous training transformation.

- Revise its Training Transformation Plan to incorporate irregular warfare, complex stabilization operations, combating WMD and information operations.

- Expand the Training Transformation Business Model to consolidate joint training, prioritize new and emerging missions and exploit virtual and constructive technologies.

Photo by Staff Sergeant Stacy L. Pearsall, U.S. Air Force.

U.S. Marines conduct urban training. The number of U.S. training facilities for urban operations and the depth of instruction have increased significantly since 2002.

Language and Cultural Skills

Developing broader linguistic capability and cultural understanding is also critical to prevail in the long war and to meet 21st century challenges. The Department must dramatically increase the number of personnel proficient in key languages such as Arabic, Farsi and Chinese and make these languages available at all levels of action and decision – from the strategic to the tactical. The Department must foster a level of understanding and cultural intelligence about the Middle East and Asia comparable to that developed about the Soviet Union during the Cold War. Current

and emerging challenges highlight the increasing importance of Foreign Area Officers, who provide Combatant Commanders with political-military analysis, critical language skills and cultural adeptness. The Military Departments will increase the number of commissioned and non-commissioned officers seconded to foreign military services, in part by expanding their Foreign Area Officer programs. This action will foster professional relationships with foreign militaries, develop in-depth regional expertise, and increase unity of effort among the United States, its allies and partners. Foreign Area Officers will also be aligned with lower echelons of command to apply their knowledge at the tactical level.

To further these language and culture goals, the Department will:

- Increase funding for the Army's pilot linguist program to recruit and train native and heritage speakers to serve as translators in the Active and Reserve Components.

DoD Photo.

This heritage speaker receives the Purple Heart medal after being wounded in Iraq. His commander stated that he was essential to all his missions. He joined the U.S. Army at 17 years of age and deployed one month after turning 18. His younger brother (age 17) also plans on enlisting to become a heritage speaker.

- Require language training for Service Academy and Reserve Officer Training Corps scholarship students and expand immersion programs, semester abroad study opportunities and inter-academy foreign exchanges.

- Increase military special pay for foreign language proficiency.

- Increase National Security Education Program (NSEP) grants to American elementary, secondary and post-secondary education programs to expand non-European language instruction.

- Establish a Civilian Linguist Reserve Corps, composed of approximately 1,000 people, as an on-call cadre of high-proficiency, civilian language professionals to support the Department's evolving operational needs.

- Modify tactical and operational plans to improve language and regional training prior to deployments and develop country and language familiarization packages and operationally-focused language instruction modules for deploying forces.

Photo by Master Sergeant James M. Bowman, U.S. Air Force.

A U.S. Army Captain from the 17th Field Artillery Brigade reviews the Arabic language with local Iraqi boys at the Al-Dawaya School. The Brigade restored the Al-Dawaya School during Operation Iraqi Freedom.

Training and Educating Personnel to Strengthen Interagency Operations

The ability to integrate the Total Force with personnel from other Federal Agencies will be important to reach many U.S. objectives. Accordingly, the Department supports the creation of a National Security Officer (NSO) corps – an interagency cadre of senior military and civilian professionals able to effectively integrate and orchestrate the contributions of individual government agencies on behalf of larger national security interests.

Much as the Goldwater-Nichols requirement that senior officers complete a joint duty assignment has contributed to integrating the different cultures of the Military Departments into a more effective joint force, the QDR recommends creating incentives for senior Department and non-Department personnel to develop skills suited to the integrated interagency environment.

The Department will also transform the National Defense University, the Department's premier educational institution, into a true National Security University. Acknowledging the complexity of the 21st century security environment, this new institution will be tailored to support the educational needs of the broader U.S. national security profession. Participation from interagency partners will be increased and the curriculum will be reshaped in ways that are consistent with a unified U.S. Government approach to national security missions, and greater interagency participation will be encouraged.

Designing an Information Age Human Capital Strategy

To compete effectively with the civilian sector for highly-qualified personnel to build the Total Force, the Department must possess both a modern *Human Capital Strategy* and the authorities required to recruit, shape and sustain the force it needs.

The new *Human Capital Strategy* focuses on developing the right mix of people and skills across the Total Force. The Department's *Human Capital Strategy* may be considered "competency-focused" and "performance-based." It is based on an in-depth study of the competencies U.S. forces require and the performance standards to which they must be developed. Each of the Military Departments will map the array of competencies and performance criteria that constitute its forces and also evaluate and improve personnel development processes to achieve those standards. Advancements, awards and compensation may then be linked to an individual's performance rather than to longevity or time-in-grade. This will better align incentives to outputs and reward excellence.

To execute the *Human Capital Strategy*, the Department will establish a single Program Executive Office responsible for the consolidated Personnel Reporting/Management System and management of the Strategy as a major defense program. Once implemented, the *Human Capital Strategy* will be integrated into a consolidated personnel tracking and management system capable of linking all Department competencies to manpower, training and education.

The Department also needs to ensure suitable promotion and development opportunities are available to attract and retain the best and brightest military and civilian personnel. The Department's career advancement philosophy should foster innovation by encouraging career patterns that develop the unique skills needed to meet new missions such as irregular warfare. New career patterns might include seconding young officers, non-commissioned officers and civil servants to work within allied and partners' militaries or ministries of defense or to serve on long-term assignments in key strategic regions of the world rather than assuming the traditional career path of multiple, short-term assignments. The Department will provide further incentives and improve advancement opportunities in key career fields, including Foreign Area Officers, trainers, advisors and linguists, as well as in other mission areas that are taking on greater importance, such as unmanned aerial vehicles and information and space operations. In addition to providing incentives for strong performance and continued service, the *Human Capital Strategy*'s shaping tools must also enable discrete, necessary force reductions as well as selective accessions when a specific skill is called for and not available within the joint force.

National Security Personnel System

The Department's civilians are unique in the U.S. Government because they are an integral part of a military organization. Consequently, like the military workforce, the Department's civilians must adapt to changing mission needs. The new

National Security Personnel System (NSPS) is designed to facilitate the effective management of the Department's 650,000 civilian personnel in the 21ˢᵗ century. The NSPS addresses three major personnel issues the Department faces: staffing the enterprise to support 21ˢᵗ century missions; using compensation to compete more effectively in the broader labor market; and providing civilian support to contingency operations. The NSPS will incorporate a labor relations system that recognizes the Department's national security mission and the need to act swiftly to execute that mission while preserving the collective bargaining rights of employees. The Department will begin its transition to the new system by training personnel to implement the new procedures. The NSPS also recognizes the importance of defense civilians and the support they provide for contingency operations. It enables civilians to perform inherently governmental functions, freeing military personnel to perform inherently military functions.

Similarly, implementing the new Department of Defense Instruction *Contractor Personnel Authorized to Accompany U.S. Armed Forces* is another step toward integrating contractors into the Total Force. The Department's policy now directs that performance of commercial activities by contractors, including contingency contractors and any proposed contractor logistics support arrangements, shall be included in operational plans and orders. By factoring contractors into their planning, Combatant Commanders can better determine their mission needs.

Taken together, measures to reconfigure the Total

Force, provide a continuum of service, build the right skills and design an information-age human capital strategy will yield a Total Force that is better able to meet the diverse challenges the United States will face in coming years.

Homecoming for pilots from Marine All Weather Fighter Attack Squadron 533 after participating in Operation Iraqi Freedom.

Quadrennial Defense Review Report

ACHIEVING UNITY OF EFFORT

The Department of Defense cannot meet today's complex challenges alone. Success requires unified statecraft: the ability of the U.S. Government to bring to bear all elements of national power at home and to work in close cooperation with allies and partners abroad. During the QDR, senior leaders considered the changes needed to enable the Department to contribute better to such unified efforts. Just as the Second World War posed immense challenges that spurred joint and combined operations within the military, today's environment demands that all agencies of government become adept at integrating their efforts into a unified strategy.

This requires much more than mere coordination: the Department must work hand in glove with other agencies to execute the National Security Strategy. Interagency and international combined operations truly are the new Joint operations. Supporting and enabling other agencies, working toward common objectives, and building the capacity of partners are indispensable elements of the Department's new missions.

Why a New Approach is Essential

The United States' experience in the Cold War still profoundly influences the way that the Department of Defense is organized and executes its mission. But, the Cold War was a struggle between nation-states, requiring state-based responses to most political problems and kinetic responses to most military problems. The Department was optimized for conventional, large-scale warfighting against the regular, uniformed armed forces of hostile states.

Today, warfare is increasingly characterized by intra-state violence rather than conflict between states. Many of the United States' principal adversaries are informal networks of non-state actors that are less vulnerable to Cold War-style approaches. At the same time, many partner nations face internal rather than external threats. Defeating unconventional enemies requires unconventional approaches. The ability to wage irregular and unconventional warfare and the skills needed for counterinsurgency, stabilization and reconstruction, "military diplomacy" and complex interagency coalition operations are essential – but in many cases require new and more flexible authorities from the Congress.

Authorities developed before the age of the Internet and globalization have not kept pace with trans-national threats from geographically

From left, Honorable Zalmay Khalizad, American ambassador to Iraq; U.S. Army General George Casey Jr., commanding general Multi-National Force-Iraq; and an Iraqi dignitary gather for the formal transfer of authority of Forward Operating Base Danger from U.S. forces to the Iraqi government in 2005. All elements of the U.S. Government are working in concert to bring stability to Iraq.

dispersed non-state terrorist and criminal networks. Authorities designed during the Cold War unduly limit the ability to assist police forces or interior ministries and are now less applicable. Adversaries' use of new technologies and methods has outstripped traditional concepts of national and international security. Traditional mechanisms for creating and sustaining international cooperation are not sufficiently agile to disaggregate and defeat adversary networks at the global, regional and local levels simultaneously.

Supporting the rule of law and building civil societies where they do not exist today, or where they are in their infancy, is fundamental to winning the long war. In this sense, today's environment resembles a challenge that is different in kind, but similar in scale, to the Cold War – a challenge so immense that it requires major shifts in strategic concepts for national security and the role of military power. Therefore, the United States needs to develop new concepts and methods for interagency and international cooperation.

Strategic and Operational Frameworks

Unity of effort requires that strategies, plans and operations be closely coordinated with partners. At the operational level, the United States must be able to prevent or disrupt adversaries' ability to plan and execute operations rather than being forced to respond to attacks after they have occurred. Adversaries using asymmetric tactics are global, adaptive and fleeting, thus analyses, decisions and actions to defeat them must also be swift. But for swift action to be fashioned and

effective, it must occur within well-coordinated strategic and operational frameworks. Authorities, procedures and practices must permit the seamless integration of Federal, state and local capabilities at home and among allies, partners and non-governmental organizations abroad.

Drawing on operational experience and lessons learned over the last four years, the QDR examined changes within and beyond the Department to strengthen unity of effort. Improved interagency and international planning, preparation and execution will allow faster and more effective action in dealing with 21st century challenges. New modes of cooperation can enhance agility and effectiveness with traditional allies and engage new partners in a common cause. Initiating efforts to better understand and engage those who support the murderous ideology of terrorists and the evolution of states at strategic crossroads will be critical.

Strengthening Interagency Operations

Increasing unity of effort to achieve the nation's security policy priorities across the agencies of the Federal Government is essential. Only with coherent, leveraged U.S. Government action can the nation achieve true unity of effort with international partners. To address more effectively many security challenges, the Department is continuing to shift its emphasis from Department-centric approaches toward interagency solutions. Cooperation across the Federal Government begins in the field with the development of shared perspectives and a better understanding of each agency's role, missions and capabilities. This will complement better understanding and closer cooperation in Washington, and will extend to execution of complex operations. To that end, the Department supports improvements to strategy development and planning within the Department and with its interagency partners.

The QDR recommends the creation of National Security Planning Guidance to direct the development of both military and non-military plans and institutional capabilities. The planning guidance would set priorities and clarify national security roles and responsibilities to reduce capability gaps and eliminate redundancies. It would help Federal Departments and Agencies better align their strategy, budget and planning functions with national objectives. Stronger linkages among planners in the Military Departments, the Combatant Commands and the Joint Staff, with the Office of the Secretary of Defense and with other Departments should ensure that operations better reflect the President's National Security Strategy and country's policy goals.

Learning from the Field

Closer relationships between parent agencies in Washington and elsewhere support increased collaboration in the field. Solutions developed in the field often have applicability to interagency cooperation at the strategic and policy levels. Long experience shows that operators, regardless of parent agency, collaborate closely when faced with common challenges in the field: they often resolve interagency concerns quickly and

seamlessly to achieve team objectives.

For the Department, joint warfighters – the Combatant Commanders and leaders of deployed joint task forces – are the primary level at which unity of effort develops. For most other agencies, the U.S. Chief of Mission in a specific country, leading an interagency Country Team, has an important field leadership role. Creating opportunities to help enable Combatant Commanders (whose purview extends across many countries) to work more collaboratively with Chiefs of Mission (who focus on only one country) is one objective. Currently, personnel in the Department of State and Department of Defense must expend considerable effort, on a case-by-case basis, to act together in support of operations. The result is that Commanders and Chiefs of Mission lose agility in the face of an adaptive adversary, fleeting targets are missed, and risks to U.S. interests and those of our partners increase.

Rescue personnel from the Los Angeles, California Fire Department, working with U.S. Coast Guard and U.S. Army personnel, search for victims of Hurricane Katrina in flooded neighborhoods in New Orleans, Louisiana.

Complex Interagency Operations Abroad

The President's National Security Presidential Directive designating the Secretary of State to improve overall U.S. Government stabilization and reconstruction efforts recognizes the challenges of achieving unity of effort for complex overseas contingencies. Although many U.S. Government organizations possess knowledge and skills needed to perform tasks critical to complex operations, they are often not chartered or resourced to maintain deployable capabilities. Thus, the Department has tended to become the default responder during many contingencies. This is a short-term necessity, but the Defense Department supports legislation to enable other agencies to strengthen their capabilities so that balanced interagency operations become more feasible – recognizing that other agencies' capabilities and performance often play a critical role in allowing the Department of Defense to achieve its mission.

Recognizing that stability, security and transition operations can be critical to the long war on terrorism, the Department issued guidance in 2005 to place stability operations on par with major combat operations within the Department. The directive calls for improving the Department's ability to work with interagency partners, international organizations, non-governmental organizations and others to increase capacities to participate in complex operations abroad. When implemented, the Department will be able to provide better support to civilian-led missions, or to lead stabilization operations when appropriate.

The QDR supports efforts to expand the expeditionary capacity of agency partners. In addition, increased coordination between geographic Combatant Commands and interagency partners in the field will increase overall effectiveness. The Department proposes a number of policy and legislative initiatives to improve unity of effort for complex interagency operations abroad, providing greater Presidential flexibility in responding to security challenges. The Department will:

- Support substantially increased resources for the Department of State's Coordinator for Reconstruction and Stability and State's associated proposal to establish a deployable Civilian Reserve Corps and a Conflict Response Fund.

- Support broader Presidential authorities to redirect resources and task the best-situated agencies to respond, recognizing that other government agencies may be best suited to provide necessary support in overseas emergencies. This new authority would enable the U.S. Government to capitalize on inherent competencies of individual agencies to tailor a more effective immediate response.

- Strengthen internal Department mechanisms for interagency coordination.

- Improve the Department's ability to assess the relative benefits of security cooperation activities to enable better resource allocation decisions.

- Strengthen the Department's regional centers to become U.S. Government assets in support of government outreach to regional opinion-makers.

Complex Interagency Operations at Home

Unified interagency efforts are no less important at home. The Department must work as part of a unified interagency effort with the Department of Homeland Security and other Federal, state and local agencies to address threats to the U.S. homeland. Moreover, the response to Hurricane Katrina vividly illustrated the need for the Department to support other agencies in the context of complex interagency operations at home.

The QDR recommends several actions to improve unity of effort with other Federal agencies, state and local governments to improve homeland defense and homeland security. The Department will:

- In partnership with Department of Homeland Security, develop a National Homeland Security Plan clarifying the optimum distribution of effort among Federal agencies for prevention, preparation and response.

- Expand training programs to accommodate planners from other agencies and, working with the Department of Homeland Security and other interagency partners, offer assistance to develop new courses on developing and implementing strategic-level plans for disaster assistance, consequence management and catastrophic events.

- Partner with the Department of Homeland Security to design and facilitate full-scope interagency homeland defense and civil support exercises, leveraging the Defense Department's experience in planning and training. The exercises will be conducted in near-real-world conditions, with civilian and military participation from national, state and local government agencies. These exercises should help to yield common understandings of assigned roles and responsibilities, and shared practice in complex planning and operations.

- At the request of the Department of Homeland Security, organize and sponsor homeland defense tabletop exercises, in which senior leaders from civilian and military agencies practice responses to disaster scenarios.

- Continue consultations with our neighbors to address security and defense issues of common concern, while ensuring coordination with the Department of Homeland Security.

Working with International Allies and Partners

Long-standing alliance relationships will continue to underpin unified efforts to address 21st century security challenges. These established relationships continue to evolve, ensuring their

U.S. and Mexican forces worked together distributing relief supplies at D'Iberville Elementary School in Mississippi following Hurricane Katrina.

relevance even as new challenges emerge. The ability of the United States and its allies to work together to influence the global environment is fundamental to defeating terrorist networks. Wherever possible, the United States works with or through others: enabling allied and partner capabilities, building their capacity and developing mechanisms to share the risks and responsibilities of today's complex challenges.

The nation's alliances provide a foundation for working to address common security challenges. NATO remains the cornerstone of transatlantic security and makes manifest the strategic solidarity of democratic states in Europe and North America. NATO is evolving through the addition of seven new allies, the Partnership for Peace Program, the creation of the NATO Response Force, the establishment of the new Allied Command Transformation, the Alliance's leadership of the International Security Assistance Force in Afghanistan and the NATO Training Mission in Iraq. In many European allied states, however, aging and shrinking populations are curbing defense spending on capabilities they need for conducting operations effectively alongside U.S. forces. In the Pacific, alliances with Japan, Australia, Korea and others promote bilateral and multi-lateral engagement in the region and cooperative actions to address common security threats. India is also emerging as a great power and a key strategic partner. Close cooperation with these partners in the long war on terrorism, as well as in efforts to counter WMD proliferation and other non-traditional threats, ensures the continuing need for these alliances and for improving their capabilities.

Defense Ministers attend a NATO-Ukraine Commission meeting during a NATO conference in Brussels, Belgium. NATO remains a key alliance as the United States faces traditional and emerging challenges.

The Department will continue to strengthen traditional allied operations, with increased emphasis on collective capabilities to plan and conduct stabilization, security, transition and reconstruction operations. In particular, the Department supports efforts to create a NATO stabilization and reconstruction capability and a European constabulary force. The United States will work to strengthen allied capabilities for the long war and countering WMD. The United States, in concert with allies, will promote the aim of tailoring national military contributions to best employ the unique capabilities and characteristics of each ally, achieving a unified effort greater than the sum of its parts.

Consistent with the President's emphasis on the need to prevent, rather than be forced to respond to, attacks, the Department recommends that the United States continue to work with its allies to develop approaches, consistent with their domestic laws and applicable international law, to disrupt and defeat transnational threats before they mature. Concepts and constructs enabling unity of effort with more than 70 supporting nations under the Proliferation Security Initiative should be extended to domains other than WMD proliferation, including cyberspace, as a priority.

To prevent terrorist attacks or disrupt their networks, to deny them sanctuary anywhere in the world, to separate terrorists from host populations and ultimately to defeat them, the United States must also work with new international partners in less familiar areas of the world.

U.S. civil affairs officers assist residents of Ramadi with registering to vote in Anbar Province, Iraq, in August 2005. Iraqis have exercised their right to democracy in increasing numbers throughout 2004 and 2005.

This means the Department must be prepared to develop a new team of leaders and operators who are comfortable working in remote regions of the world, dealing with local and tribal communities, adapting to foreign languages and cultures and working with local networks to further U.S. and partner interests through personal engagement, persuasion and quiet influence – rather than through military force alone. To support this effort, new authorities are needed. During the Cold War the legal authorities for military action, intelligence, foreign military assistance

and cooperation with foreign police and security services were separately defined and segregated from each other. Today, there is a need for U.S. forces to transition rapidly between these types of authorities in an agile and flexible manner, to meet the challenges of the 21st century.

Based on operational experiences of the last four years, the QDR recommends that Congress provide considerably greater flexibility in the U.S. Government's ability to partner directly with nations in fighting terrorists. For some nations, this begins with training, equipping and advising their security forces to generate stability and security within their own borders. For others, it may entail providing some assistance with logistics support, equipment, training and transport to allow them to participate as members of coalitions with the United States or its allies in stability, security, transition and reconstruction operations around the globe.

Recent legislative changes remove some of the impediments to helping partners engaged in their own defense, but greater flexibility is urgently needed. The Department will seek to:

- Establish a Defense Coalition Support Account to fund and, as appropriate, stockpile routine defense articles such as helmets, body armor and night vision devices for use by coalition partners.

- Expand Department authority to provide logistics support, supplies and services to allies and coalition partners, without reimbursement as necessary, to enable coalition operations with U.S. forces.

- Expand Department authority to lease or lend equipment to allies and coalition partners for use in military operations in which they are participating with U.S. forces.

- Expand the authorities of the Departments of State and Defense to train and equip foreign security forces best suited to internal counter-terrorism and counter-insurgency operations. These may be non-military law enforcement or other security forces of the government in some nations.

The Department will continue to support initiatives, such as the Global Peace Operations Initiative, to increase the capacity of international organizations so that they can contribute more effectively to the improvement of governance and the expansion of civil society in the world. In this regard, the Department supports the African Union's development of a humanitarian crisis intervention capability, which is a good example of an international organization stepping up to the challenge of regional stabilization missions. The Department stands ready to increase its assistance to the United Nations Department of Peacekeeping Operations in areas of the Department's expertise such as doctrine, training, strategic planning and management.

Transforming Foreign Assistance

Foreign military assistance missions during the Cold War were largely designed to shore up friendly regimes against external threats. Today, the aim is for partners to govern and police

themselves effectively. Assistance in today's environment relies on the ability to improve states' governance, administration, internal security and the rule of law in order to build partner governments' legitimacy in the eyes of their own people and thereby inoculate societies against terrorism, insurgency and non-state threats. In partnership with the State Department and others, the Department must become as adept at working with foreign constabularies as it is with externally-focused armed forces, and as adept at working with interior ministries as it is with defense ministries – a substantial shift of emphasis that demands broader and more flexible legal authorities and cooperative mechanisms.

Bringing all the elements of U.S. power to bear to win the long war requires overhauling traditional foreign assistance and export control activities and laws. These include foreign aid, humanitarian assistance, post-conflict stabilization and reconstruction, foreign police training, International Military Education and Training (IMET) and, where necessary, providing advanced military technologies to foreign allies and partners. In particular, winning the long war

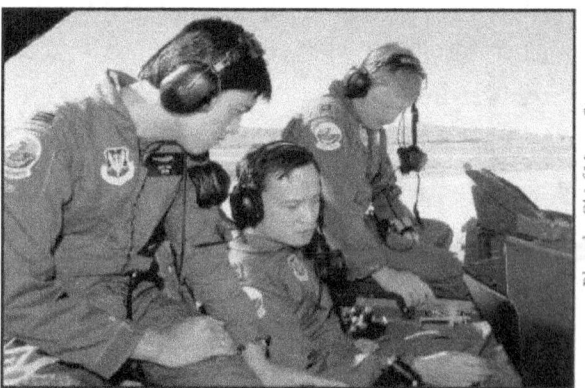

Photo by Chief Master Sergeant Don Sutherland, U.S. Air Force.

U.S. Captain John Hart (right) instructs members of the Royal Thai Air Force on the instrument panel of an F-16 Fighting Falcon as part of the International Military Education and Training program.

requires strengthening the Department's ability to train and educate current and future foreign military leaders at institutions in the United States. Doing so is critical to strengthening partnerships and building personal relationships. In all cases, they are integral to successful irregular warfare operations.

For example, quick action to relieve civilian suffering, train security forces to maintain civil order and restore critical civilian infrastructure denies the enemy opportunities to capitalize on the disorder immediately following military operations and sets more favorable conditions for longer term stabilization, transition and reconstruction. Full integration of allied and coalition capabilities ensures unity of effort for rapidly evolving counterinsurgency operations. Similarly, foreign leaders who receive U.S. education and training help their governments understand U.S. values and interests, fostering willingness to unite in a common cause.

The QDR found that, with the exception of legislation applicable only to operations in Afghanistan and Iraq, existing authorities governing planning, financing and use of these instruments for shaping international partnerships do not accommodate the dynamic foreign policy demands of the 21st century. Based on recent operational experience, the Department seeks a continuum of authorities from Congress balancing the need to act quickly in the war on terrorism with the need to integrate military power to meet long-term, enduring foreign policy objectives.

The Department recommends a number of important legislative changes in the near term, while also working in close partnership with the Department of State and the Congress to enable better alignment of the Foreign Assistance Act and the Arms Export Control Act with today's security challenges. In addition to expanding coalition management authorities, the Department seeks to:

- Institutionalize OIF/OEF authorities to conduct Humanitarian Assistance and Stability Operations.

- Significantly improve and increase IMET-like opportunities targeted at shaping relationships and developing future foreign leaders.

- Consider whether the restrictions on the American Service Members Protection Act (ASPA) on IMET and other foreign assistance programs pertaining to security and the war on terror necessitate adjustment as we continue to advance the aims of the ASPA.

- Expand the Counter Terrorism Fellowship Program beyond its current focus on senior-level government officials and national strategic issues. Combatant Commanders and U.S. Chiefs of Mission, in consultation with regional partners, will develop education programs to improve regional counter-terrorism campaigns and crisis response planning at the operational level.

Strategic Communication

Victory in the long war ultimately depends

on strategic communication by the United States and its international partners. Effective communication must build and maintain credibility and trust with friends and foes alike, through an emphasis on consistency, veracity and transparency both in words and deeds. Such credibility is essential to building trusted networks that counter ideological support for terrorism.

Responsibility for strategic communication must be government-wide and the QDR supports efforts led by the Department of State to improve integration of this vital element of national power into strategies across the Federal Government. The Department must instill communication assessments and processes into its culture, developing programs, plans, policy, information and themes to support Combatant Commanders that reflect the U.S. Government's overall strategic objectives. To this end, the Department will work to integrate communications efforts horizontally across the enterprise to link information and communication issues with broader policies, plans and actions.

The QDR identified capability gaps in each of the primary supporting capabilities of Public Affairs, Defense Support to Public Diplomacy, Military Diplomacy and Information Operations, including Psychological Operations. To close those gaps, the Department will focus on properly organizing, training, equipping and resourcing the key communication capabilities. This effort will include developing new tools and processes for assessing, analyzing and delivering information to key audiences as well as improving linguistic skills and cultural competence. These primary supporting communication capabilities will be developed with the goal of achieving a seamless communication across the U.S. Government.

U.S. soldiers with the Parwan Provincial Reconstruction Team discuss future quality of life improvements with village elders during a humanitarian aid mission to Jegdalek, Afghanistan.

Summary

The United States will not win the war on terrorism or achieve other crucial national security objectives discussed in this Report by military means alone. Instead, the application of unified statecraft, at the Federal level and in concert with allies and international partners, is critical. In addition to coalition- and partner-supported combat and preventive operations, simultaneous effective interaction with civilian populations will be essential to achieve success. Authorities that permit nimble and adaptive policies, processes and institutions – domestic and international – are essential adjuncts to the military capability needed to address the rapidly evolving security challenges around the globe.

CHAIRMAN OF THE JOINT CHIEFS OF STAFF

WASHINGTON, D.C. 20318-9999

MEMORANDUM FOR THE SECRETARY OF DEFENSE

Subject: Chairman's Assessment of the 2006 Quadrennial Defense Review

1. In accordance with title 10, United States Code, Section 118, I forward my assessment of the 2006 Quadrennial Defense Review for inclusion in the report.

2. This review was strengthened by an open and inclusive approach, which resulted in comprehensive and insightful recommendations that will guide our efforts in the coming years.

VR / *[signature]*

PETER PACE
General, United States Marine Corps
Chairman
of the Joint Chiefs of Staff

Attachment
As Stated

Chairman's Assessment

Chairman's Assessment of the 2006 Quadrennial Defense Review

Introduction

The Department of Defense conducted the 2006 Quadrennial Defense Review (QDR) during a demanding time for our Armed Forces. We are fighting a War on Terrorism of long duration while helping to foster fledgling democracies in Iraq and Afghanistan. At the same time, we are engaging nations around the world to build relationships, enhance regional stability, and strengthen deterrence – all while fundamentally transforming our military forces to defeat dangerous threats that may emerge in the decades ahead.

These concurrent challenges shaped a QDR process that balanced the needs of the ongoing struggle with longer term requirements to enhance security in a rapidly changing world. The report provides specific recommendations to transform the Department, its processes, and its forces, to meet this challenge. Success in this effort was due to the sustained leadership of senior civilians and uniformed officers, and the hard work of thousands of men and women in the Department of Defense, who together created an open, collaborative environment that permitted diversity of input, discussion, and analysis.

The QDR Process

The 2006 QDR was the first contemporary defense review to coincide with an ongoing major conflict. This compelled the Department to recast its view of future warfare through the lens of long duration conflict with its extended stabilization campaign. As a consequence, this review required a judicious balance between present needs and future capabilities. The aim was a review that was strategy driven, capabilities focused, and budget disciplined.

Benefiting from legislative relief granted by the Congress, the Department enjoyed additional time to organize, deliberate on, and craft the review. The Secretary, recognizing the opportunity for a broader spectrum of participation, directed an open and collaborative review from the beginning, soliciting input from across the Department and the interagency, as well as diverse perspectives from a variety of independent study groups. Consequently, the thoroughness, the scope of issues considered, and the level of senior leader involvement proved unprecedented.

Assessment

Any attempt to predict the future security environment of 2025 is inherently difficult. Consider the challenge in 1985 of trying to characterize the security environment that would exist in 2006. Given the dynamics of change over time, we must develop a mix of agile and flexible capabilities to mitigate uncertainty.

This review articulates a vision for the transformed force fully consistent with the demands of the anticipated security environment in 2025. To meet the key challenges in this period, we must: shape and sustain our Armed Forces to most effectively fight the War on Terrorism, transform "in stride" during wartime, strengthen our joint warfighting, and improve the quality of life of our Service members and their families.

The varied recommendations of the QDR promise to more effectively and efficiently align strategy and resources. The report outlines a force more capable of engaging in irregular warfare, and special operations forces more focused on those tasks they are best suited to perform. It foresees the need to establish long range and long loiter capabilities for strike and surveillance as well as increased littoral and undersea warfare capabilities. Finally, it strengthens deterrence options and enhances the capability to respond to catastrophic events in the homeland, whether man made or natural.

Winning the War on Terrorism

The QDR properly focuses on the War on Terrorism as our first priority. We will enhance our expeditionary combat power and shape the Services to be lighter, yet more lethal, more sustainable and more agile. We will train additional Special Operations Forces and enable traditional ground forces to conduct foreign training and security missions in addition to combat operations. This expansion allows SOF to undertake longer duration, high intensity tasks and augments the irregular warfare capability of the entire force.

A renewed emphasis on Human Intelligence, increased airborne surveillance and airlift capacity, and specialized naval forces configured for coastal and riverine operations further complement irregular warfare capacity. Additionally, the QDR recognizes Stability, Security, Transition, and Reconstruction (SSTR) as a U.S. government wide mission of increasing importance and identifies military support to SSTR as a core mission.

Finally, by emphasizing greater cultural awareness and language skills, the QDR acknowledges that victory in this long war depends on information, perception, and how and what we communicate as much as application of kinetic effects. These cultural and language capabilities also enhance effectiveness in a coalition setting during conventional operations.

Accelerating Transformation

The QDR identifies many areas and technologies that promise to revolutionize the future force. However, transformation is as much a mindset and culture as it is a technology or a platform. The QDR recognizes that we maximize the impact of our military power through closer coordination within the Department of Defense and with our interagency and international partners. Building partnership capacity invigorates our efforts and acknowledges that future challenges can be met only through the integrated use of all of the instruments of national power and through the relevant contributions of our international partners. The proposed National Security Planning Guidance promises to significantly improve national and international efforts to prevent, as well as respond to, crises at home and abroad.

The QDR takes positive steps to posture the Department's contribution to our national Homeland Defense effort. For example, several QDR initiatives dramatically improve our ability to detect threats in the approaches and interdict them at a distance. Moreover, military assistance to civil authorities, such as the response to a natural disaster, proved instrumental in shaping several QDR decisions.

Finally, the QDR envisions a wide range of initiatives that augment our capacity to shape the behavior of potential adversaries and to react to dangerous WMD related contingencies. These initiatives include acquiring more flexible conventional deterrence capabilities, solidifying the Department's WMD command and control structure, increasing the number of forces available for overseas nuclear render safe operations, and shortening their response time.

Strengthening Joint Warfighting

Integrating advanced capabilities to improve joint war fighting is at the heart of the QDR effort. We will measure resource related decisions against that goal, as we transition from an interoperable to an interdependent force, whose diverse capabilities are rapidly integrated to achieve desired effects. This applies to the full range of combat tasks as well as to evolving roles and missions in Homeland Defense, Humanitarian Assistance, and military support to Stability, Security, Transition, and Reconstruction operations.

Change must extend beyond the forces in the field to include command and control headquarters. Key is the initiative to organize, man, train, and equip selected Service headquarters to make them Joint Task Force (JTF) capable, available and ready to command and control designated Joint force missions. The existence of a trained and ready pool of JTF capable headquarters will assure a wider range of military response options.

Finally, the Defense enterprise must be reformed to create and leverage the same agility as the force it enables. QDR recommendations to implement a comprehensive Human Capital Strategy, develop more integrated and streamlined acquisition processes, and improve Strategic Communication reflect the necessary enterprise approach to building a more effective and efficient organization, freeing resources for other transformational efforts.

Improve the Quality of Life of our Service Members and our Families

Superbly trained, equipped, and highly dedicated people have always been America's ultimate advantage. Our foremost duty, and that which this QDR acknowledged in every recommendation, is the imperative of supporting our Soldiers, Sailors, Airmen, and Marines by giving them the finest equipment and training, so that they can achieve victory and return home safely.

Achieving that goal requires the proper shaping of the Total Force to sustain the Global War on Terrorism with enough force depth and critical skills to allow sufficient time for rest and refit between combat assignments. It also means more fully integrating support systems to deliver first class administrative services, supplies, and support programs for our professionals and their families.

Finally, improving the quality of life of our service members means that we will provide educational opportunities to our people, to help them realize their professional goals and personal aspirations. When their time of uniformed service is over, they will return home as outstanding citizens and role models, ready to serve our society in new and different ways.

Assessment of Risk

We cannot accurately characterize the security environment of 2025; therefore, we must hedge against this uncertainty by identifying and developing a broad range of capabilities. Further, we must organize and arrange our forces to create the agility and flexibility to deal with unknowns and surprises in the coming decades. This review has carefully balanced those areas where risk might best be taken in order to provide the needed resources for areas requiring new or additional investment.

Today, the Armed Forces of the United States stand fully capable of accomplishing all the objectives of the National Defense Strategy: securing the United States from direct attack, securing strategic access and retaining global freedom of action, strengthening alliances and partnerships, and establishing favorable security conditions. The recommendations contained in this report provide future capability, capacity, and flexibility to execute these assigned missions, while hedging against the unknown threats of 2025.

Assessment of Roles and Missions

The Department continues to refine and improve the way capabilities are developed, fielded, and integrated, in order to execute the full range of missions the Armed Forces may be called on to perform. The 2006 QDR stresses an integrated approach with interagency and international partners. This review examined the challenges of the 21st century and the responsibilities of our Armed Forces in meeting them, and found roles and missions to be fundamentally sound. I concur with this assessment.

Moving Forward

We are at a critical time in the history of this great country and find ourselves challenged in ways we did not expect. We face a ruthless enemy intent on destroying our way of life and an uncertain future security environment. The War on Terrorism – a war of long duration – differs from the kind of conflict for which the Department traditionally prepared. Our focus is increasingly on the search for small cells of terrorists and on building the capacity of our partners. However, we must also retain the capability to conduct sustained conventional combat operations and to protect the homeland.

We must prevail now while we prepare for the future. This demands a wide range of military capabilities, superbly trained forces, and increased Joint, interagency, and coalition integration.

The recommendations of this report address the current fight and the full range of missions prescribed in the National Defense Strategy, while hedging against an uncertain future. The 2006 QDR tackles the most pressing needs of the Department in a strategically sound and fiscally responsible manner. As a result our Armed Forces stand ready to protect the United States, prevent conflict and surprise attack, and prevail against adversaries wherever they may be found.

I appreciate the efforts of all who were involved in this process. I endorse the 2006 QDR and its vision of a future force – more agile and more flexible, better prepared to deal with a dynamic security environment. Our challenges are many, but the course is clear.

www.ingramcontent.com/pod-product-compliance
Lightning Source LLC
Chambersburg PA
CBHW080305290526
45790CB00005B/1940